Front Row Gal

a memoir by

BARBARA LA VALLEUR

ACCOLADES

Barbara's ability to describe subtle nuances allows readers to remember while we may not have everything go our way, there is perfection in the way we choose to come out on the other end.

–Kim Kane, award-winning author,
Sparkle On...Women Aging in Gratitude

… an epic life, a most readable experience, this book is a revelation.

–Nancy Edmonds Hanson, journalist, author

…a helluva writer…

–Clara L. Adams-Ender, Retired Brig. Gen.
US Army Nursing Corps

Knowing Barbara for many years, it is a pleasure to really get to know her inspirational life story of how she forges through disappointments and finds herself in the front row living a miraculous life that we all can learn from. I love this book!

–Tonja Waring

ACKNOWLEDGEMENTS

Every time I watch an award show like the Oscars, I think the winners need to stop thanking every single person in their lives. So, I'll keep this short.

Thank you to every single person I've known in my life, both living and dead. You made a difference and helped shape who I am.

Of special mention are my close family members: Arnie Bigbee, Andrea La Valleur-Purvis, Claire (La Valleur-Purvis) Shaw, and Dr. June La Valleur and those who are no longer living: my mother, Elva Belle (Crouch, La Valleur) Evander; my second father, Loyd Evander, and my dad, Bud La Valleur, and my sister, Sharon (La Valleur) Henneman plus my grandparents and all my aunts and uncles. With special mention and thanks to my dear, dear friend, the late Linda Hutchinson.

Patti Lustig, my productivity coach for the last four years, Michele True, my editor, and Tonja Waring, Manifest Publishing. I really couldn't have done it without you three powerful women. Thank you!

DEDICATION

The journey of a thousand miles
begins with one step.

Lao Tzu

To all those who have thought
about writing your memoir: Go for it!

TABLE OF CONTENTS

CHAPTER 1

Carefree Childhood:
Until it Wasn't

*You don't write because you want to say something,
you write because you have something to say.*

F. Scott Fitzgerald

As a kid, I was certainly not shy. My mother told me I craved attention at an early age. She said I was making people laugh by the time I was two.

I didn't have a physical security blanket when I was young. Instead, I learned that humor was my friend. In a way, it became my security blanket. It's how I learned to be accepted. It's how I learned to have people like me. It's how I learned to make friends. Most of all, it was how I learned to get attention.

Funny, I never thought about it like that at the time. I always felt secure in my place in our family. I knew that I was loved by both parents and both sisters. Everyone in our family knew I was my father's favorite, although I still don't know why. Perhaps, it was because he was a jokester himself and I made him laugh.

Mother told the story about the time I got away from her at a church event in our small hometown of Ashby in rural west central Minnesota. The population in 1945 was 425 people and it's not much more than that today. When I was two years old, evidently, I took my clothes off and ran naked down main street before she caught up with me.

My childhood, at least up to the age of twelve, was quite idyllic. Our farm was about two hundred and eighty acres, so we had enough room to explore the creek that ran behind the woods and pick wildflowers in a small area near our neighbors, the Deweys. Every spring we would walk barefoot through the damp culvert below the gravel road to the north. We squealed with delight when the cool, black mud squished between our toes. The *we* would be my sister, Sharon, and me. Sharon was two years older. June, who was two years older than Sharon, would never have dreamed of doing that.

I don't remember June being a child. She was always so grown up. I used to say, "June was born and then she was an adult." Later in life, I learned that was because our mother was sick a lot and June had to take care of us.

Sharon and I were very close. We both had ponies and belonged to the Riders Club. Sharon's pony was called Mitzi. She was a beautiful half Arabian and half Trakehner. My smaller pony, a Shetland stallion, was called Spot for his huge black and white markings.

We rode our ponies bareback walking, but often trotting or galloping the three miles into town and back in summer to train and compete with other riders from the area that belonged to the Riders Club. In the winter, the Riders Club met monthly to square dance. That was so much fun with people from five to eighty-five dancing together and laughing

My biggest conflict growing up had to do with my sisters who didn't always get along with each other. I got along with Sharon. I got along with June. But they didn't appear to me to like each other when we were kids. I always felt caught in the middle. Thankfully, they grew to love and respect each other as adults.

Another sweet memory as a child was spending time with our cousins. We had eleven cousins on the La Valleur side of the family. The Bowmans lived close by, so it was always fun to go to Aunt Goldie's and eat her incredible homemade cinnamon rolls. The Mahars lived in southern Minnesota, so we didn't see them as often. They usually came in the summer months and again at Christmas. That's when all the cousins and our parents would go to Grandpa John's and Grandma Mabel's house where we laughed, played games, and sang carols. We always sang a lot together, especially when my dad's younger sister, Aunt Gloria, was there. She eventually became a professional singer-songwriter and entertainer traveling the country and performing everywhere she went. She had a sweet voice.

One memory stands out from one of Aunt Gloria's visits. It was 1952. Mother and I were at my grandparent's farm about five miles from where we lived. Aunt Goldie and Aunt Gloria (who incidentally grew up in that house) plus my Grandma Mabel, were there. The four women were playing canasta. Mother was partnered with Aunt Gloria and Aunt Goldie was with Grandma.

When playing partners in canasta, two decks are used. The "pile" can build up, especially if someone has played a wild card to "freeze" the pack. That is what had happened in this game.

I was fascinated as I stood behind Aunt Gloria watching and trying to figure out the rules of the game. So, when Grandma played a queen to Aunt Gloria (who had four queens in her hand), Aunt Gloria picked up the pile making canastas and scoring lots of points. But something puzzled me.

As Aunt Gloria laid down her discard to Aunt Goldie, two queens remained in her hand. Being the inquisitive child I was, I asked innocently, "Aunt Gloria, why didn't you play the other two queens you have in your hand?"

There was an audible gasp. All eyes, raised in surprise at my revelation, turned to stare at me. I realized I had made a serious mistake divulging that secret. No one said a word. But I soon found myself banished to another room. The next day, my mother taught me how to play canasta. I was seven years old.

Our cousins on my mother's side, her sister, my Aunt Alethea, and her husband, Uncle Tex, lived in southern California. Back in the 1950s we looked forward to their annual two-week summer visits. The highlight was always taking the old pontoon out to fish and swim.

Eagle Lake is a pristine, spring-fed lake and one of only two lakes in Minnesota that contains freshwater coral. That pontoon boat, made by Grandpa John, was constructed with old barrels and wooden slats with chicken wire on three sides. The back was open with a two-foot square cut out for the small outboard motor. We had such fun on the old pontoon every summer when the Kerseys came. We'd hang over the back edge of the pontoon and play in the water. We had a makeshift chamber pot, an old white enamel bucket was situated in the corner if we had to use the toilet since we were out for hours at a time. Two of the cousins held up a blanket or a towel for privacy.

It was always a sad day to see the Kerseys drive off in their 1956 red and white Chevy as they headed back home to California.

Growing up on the farm in the 1950s, it was normal to babysit for the neighbor's children. I shudder to think of the immense responsibilities I had babysitting a newborn baby on a farm, miles from town or our farm. The parents would stay out for hours in the evening. There were no cellphones back then if anything went wrong. I was only ten years old!

Being raised on a farm and seeing animals being born and, sometimes, dying, I learned to accept life and death as a natural occurrence. There wasn't much that frightened me. But I do remember being scared to go up the stairs to our bedroom when I was in grade school. There was a window on the landing, and I used to be frightened that someone was going to shoot an arrow in my back as I walked up the stairs. That was why I always ran up the stairs to our bedrooms – especially at night.

Even as a child, I had a secret desire to be accepted and acknowledged. Perhaps it was because my oldest sister was always the best at everything she did. I distinctly remember being embarrassed as I sat in the gym next to our mother at June's high school graduation. She received *every* award open to girls in her class except salutatorian. And that was only because she was already valedictorian. It was super hard to live up to her reputation. I know it was even harder for Sharon, who followed June so closely. Everyone expected Sharon and me to be "another June." Well, we weren't.

One of my favorite teachers in grade school was Mrs. Vida Hoff because, in addition to having a grandmotherly nature about her, she would take a half hour each afternoon to read to us eventually covering all of Laura Ingles Wilder books about life on the prairie. They were filled with riveting adventures.

Another teacher who was funny, even though I'm certain she didn't realize it, was Mrs. Irene Norby. She was my English teacher in seventh and eighth grades. She was a neighbor north of us on the gravel road. She just seemed quirky, and we made fun of her unmercifully behind her back. Kids will be kids, I guess.

Only two teachers, Mrs. Agnes Howard, a home economics teacher and advisor for Camp Fire Girls, and Mr. Gunderson (he was only known by his last name), the sixth-grade teacher, influenced me in negative ways. Sharon had been in Mr. Gunderson's class the previous year and they butted heads all year long. Sharon was unfairly treated by him as a result and the following year I was dealt the consequences.

He refused to have me in his class. As a result, the class was divided. Boys in one room and girls in another room. Everyone blamed me for that divide, so I had a rough first few weeks of sixth grade. Interesting to wonder how that would pan out today with the *Me Too, Movement*. No one blamed Mr. Gunderson, of course. However unfair it was, I felt responsible and sad for a long time that the boys and girls of our class were separated.

The Mrs. Howard fiasco occurred when I was ten and belonged to a group called Camp Fire Girls. Our group met after school in the Home Economics Room. There were about fifteen of us. On this day, we were all seated in a large circle, excited to play a game.

Mrs. Howard was our club advisor. First, she explained the rules and walked around the outside of the circle whispering in each girl's ear the name of an animal. At the sound of one-two-three we had been told to shout out as loudly as we could, the sound made by each animal she had assigned us. When she got to me, she whispered, "cow."

Now, I'm someone who loves playing games, so I was ready to give it my all and at the count of three, I yelled at the top of my voice, "Mooooooooooo!" Much to my horror, Mrs. Howard had whispered in the ears of each of the other girls, "Be quiet. Don't say anything." So, I was the only one who belted out the animal sound. I sat mortified while all my friends and Mrs. Howard laughed and laughed and laughed.

I firmly believe the teacher had singled me out as punishment for something June had done months earlier.

June was a straight "A" student. So, when Mrs. Howard gave her a "C" on her report card, June stood her ground and questioned the grade. She asked Mrs. Howard how she could possibly receive a "C" on her report card when she'd received "A's" on all the tests and all the assignments for that term. Even then, June was strong and stood up for herself as our mother had taught all of us.

Mother went in to talk with Mrs. Howard about the grade and to get an explanation for why she gave June a "C" given every test and course grade had an A. I wasn't present for that conversation, but I do remember that Mrs. Howard begrudgingly revised June's grade to an "A." June would go on to become Valedictorian of her senior class. But I would assert that Mrs. Howard never forgot her own humiliation for being "caught" by a student and her parent in a case of unjustifiable bias.

The Camp Fire Girl experience remains the most embarrassing moment of my life.

Defining Moment:
Humor is my security blanket.

Lesson Learned:
You can be remembered for making people laugh or cry. I chose to make people laugh.

CHAPTER 2

Two Fathers

This is a theme I wrote for an English class as a junior at Battle Lake High School. I was seventeen years old. My English teacher, Miss Vivian Ramberg, whom I credit with teaching me the love of the English language, gave me the grade of A/B. The A was for writing and content, the B was for grammar. There is a reference to my father's suicide which I address in later chapters.

Barbara La Valleur

Theme I
Teacher's grade: A/B
Teacher's note: Beautiful tribute.
I'm really moved! VR

Having two fathers is usually not considered desirable, but in my case, it couldn't have been better.

Maybe it was because he named me, maybe because we were so much alike, but whatever the reason, I was my father's "pet." We always seemed to get along better than usual. There were incidents when he became angry with me, like the time I got a new toothbrush and spent the better part of the afternoon brushing my teeth – which caused him to burn the toothbrush – because I had used up a whole tube of toothpaste, but it's only normal to get angry at times.

It seems to me he was forever laughing and happy. Playing jokes on people was a favorite of his. At a party my folks had one New Year's Eve, he had gotten a "party pooper" (a flat red, rubber balloon filled with air) and placed it under a chair cushion. One could imagine the embarrassment and the laughter.

Dad loved hunting and being outdoors. It was no great surprise to anyone when I asked to go along with the men and boys. Usually, I was permitted to tag along, though I don't remember ever shooting a thing, even though I had taken gun safety in elementary school. If Dad went out in the field to plow, I'd go along. He let me uncover the corn that had been plowed over. Always making me feel needed was one of the things I liked about him. It made me feel so important. When I finally got to wear bib overalls (just like Dad's), I felt as if I had reached my biggest goal.

All the memories I have of my father are good ones. It's only natural to remember the good things and forget the bad. The last few months of my dad's life were miserable for him, and it was a time I don't recall being pleasant for the family either. Mental illness is never a pleasant memory, especially when it hits someone you love. So, I will always remember him as my happy, fun-loving father.

At first, life without Dad was disastrous. I had a difficult time adjusting to it. New changes were in store for the La Valleur family. When Mother told us that we would have to sell the farm, I cursed my dead father. When you must move from the only place you have ever lived, it's hard to take – especially when you're only twelve-years-old! Adjusting to town life was much easier than I had anticipated. After a short period, town was "the only place to live."

In little more than a year, we were in for another shock—at least us kids. We had to move to another town so Mother could set up her hair salon business. I guess I had always thought I'd grow up, marry, have children, and die right in Ashby, Minnesota. Moving was the end of everything for me at that time.

We finally got settled in Battle Lake and I literally loathed it at first. Within a few months, life was worth living again.

All this time, I was coming closer to my mother. She had a double role as mother and father to the three of us. Living in the tiny apartment and with mother working, we had to get along, and we did.

When you have had something and lost it, you never realize how lucky you were until it is too late. It angered me to see friends treat their parents with disrespect. I was infuriated when my friends took their parents for granted.

It was now more than two years since the death of my father. We all missed having a man around the house and after a while, Mother began to look for someone to share the rest of her life with her and us.

I didn't know Loyd well at all. At the wedding ceremony, I felt funny. My mother was marrying a man I hardly knew. It wasn't because I hadn't seen him enough, but he was quiet—he said very little. I agree that it is tough for a man to get a word in when there are four women talking all the time, but with Loyd, I deemed it impossible for him. He was so shy and opposite to my own father, I didn't see how things could ever work out. But I was happy for mother.

One of the nicest things my new father had done was to build a new house for us. It was fabulous. None of us had ever lived in a new house before and to me, it was a tremendous thrill. But I still didn't *know* Loyd.

I'll have to admit I was jealous of him at first because mother no longer gave all her attention to us. It hurt a little, but not for long.

Trying to get Loyd to talk was like opening a fresh can of coffee with your teeth. Impossible! But as time went on, the ice began to thaw. At times, he'd even talk! But that was only at times.

Can you imagine how frightened the innocent bachelor must have been to have fallen onto these four loquacious women? No wonder the fellow clamped up. Looking back, I can laugh with a little sympathy for him–he must have had a lot of courage.

They say that a woman should never expect to change her husband, but there are usually some exceptions to the rule. This was undoubtedly an exception. There was almost a complete change. To someone who isn't a party goer, some parties can be frightening, but Loyd has done extremely well. We like parties and going places. Loyd can be persuaded to attend them if we twist his arm. We were very proud we convinced him to wear a suit twice in two years!! (Once was at his own wedding and last week at an open house for a newly married couple.)

But seriously, though Loyd has changed quite a bit these past two years, he hasn't lost any of the original good traits he brought into the marriage. He is truly a fine, trustworthy, and intelligent man. We're a family once again and I'm proud of my family. We can have a relaxing game of Scrabble or cards at home instead of going someplace else to have fun. I enjoy staying home much more now than going out.

I didn't realize until later, that the reason Loyd fit in so well was because he *wasn't* like my own father. I am glad he wasn't. Perhaps, if they had been similar, I would have compared the two all my life. With Loyd, it was impossible. I've never met a man like him before and I probably never will again either.

I can't help but believe I have been doubly blessed by having twice as much as usual having two tremendous fathers instead of one, and I'm truly thankful.

Defining Moment:
Change brings new opportunities.

Lesson Learned:
Having two fathers worked for me.

NOTE: Mother and Loyd were married over thirty years and made a good life together combining their workspaces before he died. Loyd built a beauty shop in the lower level of their home where she was able to continue working as a hairdresser for several years.

After she retired, he turned the back room into a makeshift studio where she put her small pottery wheel and would spend hours creating small vases and tiny bowls. Loyd continued his family business of running Camp Roma on Eagle Lake, MN just off Highway 78.

I worked for Loyd during the summers of my high school years doing all kinds of things from cleaning the eight cabins and a central shower and toilet building to catching frogs and digging grub worms to sell to fishermen who came to Camp Roma.

Loyd's small store was the only place on the lake to buy staple groceries, fishing licenses, and ice to put their fish on for their long drives home to South Dakota, Iowa, Illinois, and Nebraska. The store was also a favorite hangout for people in the evening to sit on the porch and tell stories about the day's catch. Exaggerations were expected.

I spent many a summer afternoon in the back room of the store playing cards with Loyd in between customers. We'd listen to WCCO radio's Halsey Hall broadcasting the Minnesota Twins games.

Loyd taught me how to play cribbage, but I never could understand Pinochle. One of my fondest memories was bringing Loyd his favorite meal of a grilled cheese sandwich and Campbell's Tomato Soup (made with milk) and sitting with him in the back room listening to him talk about the "good ole days." He was a brilliant, self-made man of many talents. He taught me a lot.

When it came time for Loyd to retire, he sold the resort to a South Dakota family, with the parents and each of their children's families having their own cabin. They, in turn, remodeled them into large, beautiful year-round homes.

CHAPTER 3

Front Row Gal

Living life in the front row is a metaphor
for what makes us come alive.

Barbara La Valleur

If only I'd had my trusty Nikon back then. All I had was a tiny silver and black Kodak Instamatic camera. Not that I was in competition with the fourteen radio and television stations and other media covering the event that day. It was a big day in San Diego. John F Kennedy was to record a major presidential address.

It was June 6, 1963, less than two weeks after I graduated from high school in my hometown of Battle Lake, Minnesota. I was a naive yet bold young woman, one of thousands waiting to hear our dashing young President with his distinctive Bostonian accent.

He was about to deliver the commencement address in the Aztec Bowl at San Diego State College, where I planned to attend college that fall. The crowd of 30,000 was clapping and whistling and, like me, full of excitement and anticipation to see and hear our hero, JFK. It was also to be a major speech about education for the nation.

What I didn't know then, was that I was about to take my first "journalistic" photos of one of the most famous people in the world.

Unfortunately, I wasn't poised for the best images–and not only because I had an inadequate camera.

Normally, I'm a front row gal, which would have set me up perfectly, especially since I only had a pathetic Instamatic. But I was happy to have scored a ticket to the event, even if it meant sitting high up on the top back bleachers in the bustling crowd that sunny summer day.

My heart was racing as I stood up with trepidation and made my way gingerly down about thirty rows of bleachers to the ground near where all the SDSC graduates were seated. Walking across the grass for about fifty yards and now full of purpose, I made my way closer to the podium where the President was speaking, ducking under a rope to get as close as possible. Within a couple of minutes, a Secret Service man came dashing over to me exclaiming, *"Hey, Lady! You're in the Press Box! You must leave. NOW!"*

I assured him I would go as soon as I was finished taking a couple more photos. Little did I realize that I had taken a firm stand that would support my future career as a successful international photojournalist. I wasn't about to let anyone, not even a U.S. Secret Service man, deter me from my intention to photograph the President. Years later, one of my bosses called me the most intentional person he'd ever met.

But I'm getting ahead of myself.

My idyllic childhood had been marred by only two major events: experiencing my first death, my grandma, at the young age of eleven and almost a year later, and worse yet, my dad died by suicide. It was Christmastime. I was twelve.

That set up a chain of events that changed everything. We had to sell our farm along with our ponies, which was devastating. It was the only place I'd ever called home. My mother went back to cosmetology school to obtain her Minnesota license so she could subsequently establish her first hair salon in a nearby town. That, of course, led to a move to Battle Lake, a rival in high school sports of my hometown of Ashby, less than twenty miles away, where I'd happily attended grade and junior high school.

The first day in my new school was unbelievably scary. I had grown up with a powerful mother and two strong older sisters, so I was blessed with a healthy dose of self-confidence. That said, as I walked into Battle Lake High School that cool September morning back in 1960, I was full of trepidation. My palms were perspiring, my throat was dry, my heart was racing. Except for my sister, Sharon, who was a junior, and nowhere to be seen, I didn't know anyone at the school.

I walked into my freshman classroom with fear in my eyes, staring at the thirty-five other students. I didn't know a soul. If I could have, I would have turned around, gone out the door, and left school. But I knew that wasn't an option and that I'd have to face my new situation sooner or later: I was the new kid in town. All the other students in my class had known each other for years since they had been together in grade school. I gulped and took a seat at a desk. The rest of the day remains a blur.

Somehow, I got through my case of the jitters on that first day of school. In a matter of a few short weeks, I'd made several friends and knew every one of my classmates by name.

It felt natural to pass notes during study hall discussing which of the top tunes we loved best. Two of my favorites were *Theme from Summer Place* by Percy Faith and *It's Now or Never* by Elvis Presley.

Almost every day after eating lunch in the school cafeteria, a small group of us would walk the four blocks downtown to buy delicious individual pies at Madsen's Bakery. They cost fifteen cents. My favorite was cherry pie. I can still envision the yummy, flaky crust and feel the sweet-sharp tang of cherries in jellied sauce. Walking back to school, we discussed upcoming football games, who would be chosen cheerleaders and what was happening in town.

Within a few weeks, I had my first serious love interest, Dean Peterson. I was fifteen, he was sixteen. He was tall, dark, and handsome. I found out he was also somewhat of an outsider, not in the *in* crowd that I was in. Of course, that made him twice as alluring to me. I enjoyed being a bit defiant and not necessarily following the pack.

One day, we were all walking to the bakery to buy our pies discussing the new, used car dealership opening in town that day. The door prize was a 1937 two-toned brown Chevy. I told my new friends that if I won, I would paint the car purple with pink polka dots. We laughed and soon we were back at school in time for afternoon classes.

That evening, the drawing was held at the new business. Since my family and I lived in an apartment downtown, only two blocks from the car dealership, my sister, Sharon, and I decided to walk down there, just for fun. Clearly, there weren't a lot of options for entertainment in our small town.

People were clustered about in groups discussing the weather and generally making small talk. There weren't as many people there as I had expected for such a big occasion. After all, it wasn't often that a new business opened in town. When it came time for the drawing, a hush passed over the entire shop floor. People were anxious, secretly hoping they'd be the one to win.

I was under no such illusion. After all, I was fifteen and I didn't have my drivers' license. And where would I get the twenty-five cents a gallon to fill the gas tank? So, when they called the winning name "Barbara La Valleur," I was beyond shocked. My eyes got big. My heart started to race. Holy cow! I'd won! A car! In

1963, the average cost of a new car was $2,600. Although it wasn't a *new* car, it was new to me. Never in my wildest dreams did I think I would own a car at my age, and I certainly didn't expect to *win* one.

What now? I couldn't drive the car out of the showroom—I can't remember who did that for me. My mother was struck speechless when we returned to the apartment that night and I told her I'd won the door prize—a car. She laughed out loud.

My win was the talk of the school the next day at lunch hour as we walked downtown to get our pies. I was beaming, thrilled to be the center of attention for the first time at my new school.

Well, I didn't paint the car purple with pink polka dots. Instead, within a few days—never having driven it—I sold it to my boyfriend, Dean, for fifty dollars. Then I took the money to the Battle Lake Review, our weekly newspaper which was located right across the street from our upstairs apartment. Richard Tampke, the editor, also sold portable typewriters. I took my car money and bought the weird-looking, small grey no brand name typewriter in its own case with a carrying handle. It was a premonition for things to come. I walked proudly back across the street carrying my new typewriter. I was in heaven.

Little did I know that winning that 1937 Chevy would launch my fabulous international photojournalism career which would span over five and a half decades.

I'm happy to report that the Battle Lake Review is still plugging away, under new ownership. They publish not only a weekly newspaper for Battle Lake, but for years, they also publish the Ashby Post, 136 years after they began publishing newspapers in 1884. But they don't sell typewriters anymore.

Not everything went my way that fall. When it came time for the annual cheerleader competition in the school gym (during what was then called a lyceum) I had the delusional thought that, because both my older sisters were always chosen cheerleaders, and because we were all athletic, that I, too, would have no problem being chosen.

I don't know if it's the same in all schools anymore, but at the time, the cheerleader election was (as they often are in school situations) a popularity contest. You didn't have to be athletic. You merely had to be known and liked. I hadn't quite *made it* into that category yet evidently. It was a devastating experience for me. To make it worse, one of the girls who would win was becoming my best friend. She was more of an intellectual, book-type person and she certainly wasn't athletic. Ouch. Privately, I shed tears when I got home. I had something to work on and was justified the following year when I *was* elected a cheerleader.

By the way, that girl, also called Barb, not only became my best friend, but we remain besties to this day, almost sixty years later.

New Year's Eve 1960 remains one of the most memorable New Year's Eves of my life – and not for the best of reasons. A group of my high school friends and I had attended a party at Sybil Deutsch's house. Our families had known each other for years. Our parents were card-playing and hunting friends. Sybil and my sister Sharon were in the same class, two years ahead of me. The Deutschs had a beautiful new home on Clitherall Lake, just south of town with a great family room in the lower level, perfect for parties.

Unfortunately, her parents kicked us all out minutes before midnight, so a small group of us got in a car, drove back to Battle Lake, and proceeded to come up with fun ideas to bring in the New Year. As we cruised up and down the unusually wide Main Street – all of two blocks – we came up with what we thought was a hilarious prank.

Butch and I were the only two freshmen in a car with three seniors: Tony, Peggy, and my new "boyfriend" who shall remain nameless for now.

Butch said he had a double row of firecrackers. So, we thought what a great way to ring in the New Year. But where should we let them off? Someone, I don't remember who, had the bright idea that we should place them in the entryway of the enclosed stairwell of a downtown business, a store named after its owner, Shorty, who lived upstairs with his wife. We didn't give a thought to the fact that Shorty's was located right across the street from a nursing home.

Butch took the firecrackers, got out of the car, lit them, and tossed them in the door of the stairwell, then ran back and jumped in the car and we drove off. Once they started pop...pop...popping we laughed our heads off and proceeded to drive back and forth on Main Street – both blocks – until the noise stopped several minutes later. We were oblivious to the fact that Shorty had come downstairs and stood outside watching us as we cruised by. After all the excitement, we went home.

The next morning, hearing a knock on our door, I opened it and began experiencing regret that would last for months. My mother and sister stood behind me as the local sheriff stood at the door. He said that I had been observed, along with three others, in a car at midnight the previous night and was suspected of being involved in a firecracker fiasco.

While I don't remember my mother's immediate response, I do remember what followed. Within days, the four of us would be summoned to a court hearing. But not my boyfriend, who was cleverly scrunched down in the middle of the back seat and to this day, he was never identified because he couldn't be seen.

Shorty had recognized the rest of us. And no one ever snitched on Norm Tegmeier. (Outed!) While we weren't officially arrested, we were all required to appear before a judge in the nearby county seat of Fergus Falls. Oh my! I remember that day as if it were yesterday.

My mother asked my grandfather to come with us, I expect for male moral support. That embarrassed me even more. I loved my grandpa and was so ashamed to disappoint him. Although he had never made me feel that way.

Because mother had a planned trip with an airline ticket to visit her parents in California on the date in January we were summoned, the court rescheduled my hearing earlier to accommodate her plans. That meant I had to go on my own without my friend's support.

As I sat across the table from the judge in between mother and grandpa, mortified that I was not with my friends, I didn't say anything – I was too terrified to speak. The judge sternly proceeded to explain why what we had done was such a serious offense.

The judge pointed out that Shorty and his wife were seniors. On a more serious note, the nursing home across the street was full of frail, at-risk elders. While our antics didn't cause physical harm to anyone that night, they could have caused someone to have a heart attack and die. My eyes got bigger and bigger as the judge spoke, and I thought about how awful *THAT* would have been. I answered his questions meekly with, "Yes, sir," and "No, sir."

After his thorough dressing down and with my admission of guilt, my punishment would be probation and curfew until the end of the school year in May. Remember, it was January. I would be on curfew and could only attend school or church functions in the evening. I had to be in by nine every night. As a fifteen-year-old who was new to dating, that was certainly grim news.

I wondered what kind of punishment my complicit mates would get when they appeared together in front of the judge the following week. As it turns out, they got the same punishment. But their experience was not nearly as terrifying as mine was since they had each other for moral support.

Suffice it to say, I learned my lesson: Think about the consequences of my actions before doing something, especially something as foolish as lighting firecrackers at midnight near a nursing home! In the end, we were all released from probation two months early for good behavior and the incident was erased from our records when we turned eighteen. Whew!

My remaining high school years were spent being as active as possible and staying out of trouble. Not surprisingly, I was co-editor with Carol Thorstenson of *The Battler*, our mimeographed school newspaper. I can still smell that distinctive alcohol, inky aroma of the mimeograph machine.

In my senior year, I worked in the principal's office for Mr. James Rude. I liked him. He liked me. I still have the charm bracelet he gave me when I graduated. Over the years, I've added: a crab for my zodiac sign, a card hand to represent my love of card-playing, a globe for my international travels, a Mexican hat, a Dutch windmill, a cluster of German grapes, an Italian gondola, the Tower of London, Picasso's one-eyed sculpture in Chicago, the four presidents of Mount Rushmore, a typewriter, tiny camera (complete with a black leather body), my National Press Photographer Association charm, a St. Thomas, US Virgin Island sailboat, a tiny White House and a "big bee" in honor of my husband, Arnie Bigbee.

Perhaps not surprisingly, my favorite class in high school was English taught by Miss Vivian Ramberg. I will forever be grateful to Miss Ramberg who taught me the love of the English language. She had a wicked sense of humor which I came to enjoy later in life. One of my fondest memories of her is when she accompanied our class for our annual senior trip. We went to Minneapolis. It was only the second time I'd been to the *big city*. That day in May, our class of thirty-six students had two choices of how we could spend the evening. We could either go to a Minnesota Twins baseball game or attend Sir Tyrone Guthrie's namesake theater, The Guthrie Theater. It was the opening week of the now world-famous theater. Two girlfriends, (Gay Prescher and Alice Talsness) Miss Ramberg, and I chose the theater. When we saw Sir Guthrie sitting down front in the audience an excited thrill ran through me. The other thirty-three went to the baseball game. I still have my program of *Hamlet* by William Shakespeare. I wonder if any of my other classmates have their program of the Twins game.

The other memory of Miss Ramberg that stands out took place years later when I lived in Europe. I never failed to call and visit her when I returned home on one of my few trips to visit my family. We drank tea and had great conversations. And we had lots of chuckles as we reminisced.

The night of high school graduation in late May 1963, I was proud to receive my diploma and to be among the top ten percent of my class. My grandparents had driven from California to attend. It was a big deal.

The next morning, I got in the back seat of Grandpa Crouch's car with alacrity. I felt like the world was my oyster as I was about to embark on a life-changing journey.

My plan was to get a summer job, probably in the Long Beach area where my aunt and cousins lived. That fall, I'd stay with my grandparents who lived in Spring Valley, California, just north of the Mexican border, until I found an apartment or dorm roommate while I attended San Diego State College. I didn't know a case of homesickness would supplant those plans a few months later.

After a long but uneventful drive across half the country, we arrived in California. The air smelled different, salty; we were close to the ocean. I'd never seen so many houses so close together. To me it was a sea of fast-food joints on every corner. I don't know whether it was because what I saw was novel, but I deemed it a very beach-centric environment: all the billboard signs, the food, the clothes were beachy. It was an eye-opening adventure, for sure.

My Aunt Aletha drove down from Lakewood, California, to pick me up as she had offered to have me stay with them that summer. She was going to help me find a job and we'd go to the beach as often as possible. It was her thing. She had leather-tanned skin from her years of beach-going. Aunt Al, as I called her, had the best sense of humor. But she could also lay down the law if her kids and I got out of hand. I'll always remember when she took me for my first interview at Tip Top # 2. Oh, my God. I was SO dang scared.

Defining Moment:
I am a front row gal.

Lesson Learned:
It's good practice to think about the
consequences of your actions on others.

CHAPTER 4

Gray Lady & Loves Lost

All the most powerful emotions come from
chaos – fear, anger, love – especially love.
Love is chaos itself. Love makes no sense.
It shakes you up and spins you around.
And then, eventually it falls apart.

Kirsten Miller

At the end of my freshman year at Moorhead State, I quit college and got married to Joe Kotnik. One of my professors, God bless her, Melva Moline, fervently tried to talk me into staying in college. Unfortunately, I didn't listen.

Several of my high school friends were getting married. I thought I should, too. Besides, I thought I was pregnant. Turns out, thankfully, I wasn't.

Joe vaguely resembled Elvis Presley with glasses. He could curl his lip and flip his hair over. He was a six feet one-inch senior history major about to start summer school. I got a job working in the Sporting Goods Department at the first Kmart in North Dakota. Standing on the concrete floor for months in that Fargo store has given me a lifetime of varicose veins. I sold everything from bowling balls to fishing lures to M1 rifles. Joe attended classes and studied for his goal of becoming a high school history and social studies teacher.

We didn't have much of a social life because we couldn't afford it. But he did promise me that if he got a teaching position the following year that was anywhere near a college or university, I could go back to further my education. That gave me hope for the future.

So, when Joe landed a job in Starbuck, a town with slightly more than a thousand residents in west-central Minnesota, I was excited. It was less than twenty miles to the Morris campus of the University of Minnesota. I must admit, the first year that he was teaching wasn't exactly how I expected my life to turn out; even though he kept saying that I would be able to go back to college, I was cautiously encouraged.

At first, we found an upstairs apartment over a local business in the center of town. A couple of months later, we rented a small house not much bigger than the popular tiny houses of today, probably about six hundred square feet. Still, it was private and quieter than the upstairs apartment. I was aware that my university schedule would be busy, but I also wanted a part-time job. So, I started looking in town for what was available.

At the time, I was amazed that the only available job in Starbuck that I found was at a family owned Five & Dime store called Williams. It paid fifty cents an hour, a pathetic wage–even in the early 1960s. I knew I was worth more than that, so I kept looking.

After a few weeks of searching, to my chagrin and disappointment, I had to accept that there were no other jobs. I changed my focus and looked for something different. That's when I landed "the perfect job."

At the local nursing home, they were looking for volunteers. That fall, I became a Gray Lady at Minnewaska Lutheran Home.

While the Gray Ladies program no longer exists, the Red Cross volunteer program that supported nursing home residents, was popular at that time.

We had smart-looking uniforms that let everyone know who and what we were. Packed away in a box somewhere, I still have my gray and white striped uniform. It has white cuffs on its short sleeves and smart-looking white epaulettes on the shoulders with a white collar and a large red cross on the left breast pocket. There was also a matching nurse-style cap with a thick red cross on the front. I felt pretty spiffy in my new uniform. Granted, it wasn't a paying job. Still, I felt better about myself volunteering for a group of senior citizens than I would have been as an underpaid salesclerk at a dime store.

I found a lack of exciting things to do in town, so the few hours I spent with nursing home residents soon became the highlight of my week. Not surprisingly, I was two or three generations younger than any of the other Gray Ladies. Most Gray Ladies were retired women. I was grateful that they accepted me and treated me well. The staff and residents of the nursing home loved our visits. I was particularly popular with the senior "gentlemen" who loved any attention, especially from one as young as me.

Weather permitting, we took the residents for walks or rolls in their wheelchairs around the area. Lake Minnewaska, a large beautiful lake within the town limits, was a few blocks away and proved to be a favorite destination with a lovely view and lots of waterfowl to watch.

We also spent time listening to the residents reminiscing about their family and past. We read to them. We played cards and dominoes. We laughed together and shared stories.

They appreciated it when we would write letters to their families and friends, which most were no longer able to do. Decades before the internet and cell phones, handwritten letters were the most popular form of communication among family and old friends – especially given the cost of long-distance calls, which were more expensive during the day at that time.

After the first few weeks as a Gray Lady, it was time to look at the curriculum at the University of Minnesota, Morris, to see what classes I wanted to take. I chose English and French classes. For decades, our family had believed that our ancestry was French Canadian.

It would be almost fifty years later that my sisters, two cousins, and I would discover something different when we drove to Iowa and discovered a graveyard out in the middle of nowhere about thirty miles east of Des Moines. It was there we learned our first ancestors on my dad's side came from France.

We found the gravestone of Gabriel La Valleur, born April 7, 1804, Arroz, La Haute-Saone, about three hours from Paris. He died November 19, 1887, in Jasper County, Iowa where he was buried in a cemetery surrounded by cornfields. It put a smile on my face when I read the tombstones on either side of Gabriel: Catherine Normand and Reine Demange, his two wives

Ironically, that was only about four hours from where I had lived in Germany for eighteen years. That's another story I'll share with you in a subsequent chapter.

Back to Starbuck. Luckily, Joe walked the few blocks to school so I could take the car to classes. Soon, I was eagerly making the half-hour drive to campus four times a week and was thrilled to be in school learning again.

My husband ate his lunch at the school cafeteria for only twenty cents a meal, a bargain even then. That was fabulous, until it wasn't. Less than two weeks later, he started complaining about the quality of the food at the school meals. Then he'd make comments like he "missed my cooking." After a few more weeks of listening to his passive-aggressive complaints, I felt guilty that I wasn't being "a good wife." Six weeks into the quarter, I quit school to be able to stay home and make his lunch.

I remember the pivotal episode before I caved to his complaints. I found myself alone, crying hysterically in a fetal position on our bedroom floor in total denial about what was happening to me. I had no power. I couldn't move.

Of course, I was miserable and soon experienced my first bout of severe depression. Given who I am today, it's hard for me to imagine that I would give up my educational goals so readily for a bloody twenty-cent meal. But what did I know? It was a different time. I was a different person. I had not learned to find my voice and my power.

All I could look forward to were my few hours a week as a Gray Lady volunteering and helping seniors at the nursing home. At least that was something positive to look forward to.

By the end of that first year of Joe's teaching, our marriage had disintegrated into a shambles of a relationship. I left him that summer and moved back to Moorhead. I got a divorce that fall.

I remember my mother coming with me to appear before the judge. He wasn't nearly as daunting as the firecracker fiasco judge. Afterward, we went out to lunch, and she handed me a copy of my birth certificate. I had just turned twenty-one.

The next few years went by quickly as I focused on adventures, travel and going back to college to obtain my degree in Mass Communications.

First, I headed out to visit my sister, Sharon, who by then was married to Larry Sweeney and had a new baby, Michael. They lived in Everett, Washington. I stayed a few months taking a position at the Kmart Jewelry Department.

At some point, Sharon and Larry introduced me to his friend Robert John Abel. He was tall, dark, handsome and drove a purple MG. Over time, I fell in love with John, as I always called him, but I was in no way ready to be married again so soon.

I wanted more adventures, so I went off to Nashville, Tennessee, with a friend and found a job at the Banner and Tennessean newspapers taking ads over the phone. People would call in, often quite emotional, as they read what they wanted printed in the paper to remember and honor their "dearly departed loved ones," a custom unknown to me and evidently popular in the South. I had worked on newspapers and rarely read printed notices like that. It was quite the experience. It was the only time in my life I was called a "Northerner" and not in a complimentary way. They were not fooled by my Midwestern accent.

I didn't last long in Nashville. I even remember a conversation on a break at work in which they were talking about "the war." Given the Vietnam war was still raging, I assumed they were referring to that war. Imagine my shock when I realized they were talking about the Civil War!

I was grateful to my high school friend, Helen Marie Hunter, who came down to Nashville to drive back to Minnesota with me. Once again, I returned to my studies at Moorhead State. Occasionally, I would receive a call from John Abel. We had great, long phone conversations. We'd talk about me coming out to Spokane. The insurmountable stumbling block: he was Catholic, and I was divorced.

But being the eternal optimist, every now and again, John would talk me into driving out for a visit. Honestly, it didn't take much talking. I would make the 1,150-mile trip on I-94, basically a straight line through North Dakota and Montana on I-90, then bearing north through Idaho past beautiful Coeur d'Alene across the border to Spokane. John was always waiting. It was so worth the long drive to be together, even for a few days.

I remember the last time I visited John. We had spent our days talking and talking. We understood and agreed that there was no future for us together. Our relationship was not to be. As I left Spokane for the last time, John followed me about 35 miles to Coeur d'Alene. We stopped and for the last time, held each other in a tight embrace. Then I turned around, got into my car, and drove off, back to Minnesota, shedding tears all the way home.

John was something. He called me a few years ago out of the blue and asked me how I was doing. He told me his wife had died. I told him I was happily married to Arnie.

I still think of him wistfully, every now and again.

Back at Moorhead, I eventually completed my four-year degree after nine years of going to school full-time, part-time, getting married, getting divorced and, oh, yes…four years after my first divorce, I married my best friend from college, Stephen Moody Anderson.

I met Steve as a freshman while he was a junior. We hung out together at Sheryl's Coffee Nook across the street from the campus gates. He was friends with Sharon, too, and had been at my wedding to Joe. When he was drafted, he was unfortunately and reluctantly sent to Vietnam to fight in a war which he absolutely didn't support.

On his tour in Vietnam, he bought my first Nikon at the military base and sent it to me, saving me a lot of money. I wrote telling him about Joe's and my divorce. We corresponded. Before he came home, he sent me a package with some beautiful silky fabric.

When he returned from overseas, we started dating. I think one of the lessons Steve had learned in Vietnam was that life is tenuous, short, unpredictable. The following year, we were planning our wedding. My mother took that lovely material he had sent from Vietnam and sewed my wedding outfit.

Our simple and intimate ceremony took place in the woods behind his parents' home outside Park Rapids, Minnesota, with a few family members and friends among the trees and songbirds.

Steve picked a lovely, small bouquet of dark blue and white wildflowers from the woods right before the ceremony. My best friend from college, Nancy Edmunds, also a staff writer at *The Forum* newspaper, was my matron of honor.

Unfortunately – or fortunately – depending how I look at it, our wedding was short-lived, ending only five months to the day on February 14th. Steve was an eccentric individual, an entomologist with Bohemian traits. He was so incredibly smart, and we always had fascinating conversations. There was nothing normal about our brief, unique marriage. Our living room contained a menagerie with a large chicken wire cage (made by my stepfather, Loyd) with about a dozen iguanas of varying sizes from twelve to thirty inches head to tail, a Tokay gecko with a nasty bite and, an aquarium-like glass container with a top, of course, which held a four-foot sleek, shiny black snake of some kind.

Steve worked at a pet shop. At Christmas, he came home with a kinkajou. If you don't know what that is (at the time I certainly didn't either) it's a monkey-like animal with a prehensile tail and loves hanging from it. He loved hanging from the warm water pipes that hung from the ceiling in our basement apartment. Unfortunately, the cute round-eyed furry "friend" was not house trained. I put my foot down after scooping up poop for two days. So, the sweet-faced kinkajou was returned to the pet shop.

After our divorce, Steve remained a dear friend who I loved, not as a lover nor a husband, but certainly as a friend.

Over thirty years later, I was happy to visit and catch up with him one afternoon in Seattle with my daughter, Andrea, who was living there at the time. He and his partner, Liz Chenowith, had six good years together before he died not long afterwards, in 2012.

Defining Moments:
Know when it's time to leave.

Lessons Learned:
It's better to have loved and lost
than never to have loved at all.

Alfred, Lord Tennyson

CHAPTER 5

Battle of the Sexes

The most important words that have helped me in
life: when things have gone right or when things have
gone wrong, are 'accept responsibility'.

Billie Jean King

The 1970s were a time fraught with workplace sexism, lewd and silly sexist jokes, and blatant chauvinism. It was a decade that saw the first women's strike for equality in the United States on August twenty-sixth, 1970.

Worse than the 1940s and 1950s, it was a perilous time for women between the sexual revolution and before feminism rose in defiance. It was a painfully, demeaning time to be a woman.

I remember buying my first copy of *Ms. Magazine* and subscribing to it immediately until I left for Europe a few years later. It lifted women and was full of fascinating stories about their accomplishments. In those days and to this day, I always turned up Helen Reddy's Grammy-winning song to full volume as I belted out, *I Am Woman.*

The Battle of the Sexes was inevitable. That is what the famous tennis match was called between Bobby Riggs, a flamboyant sexist former tennis player, and Billy Jean King, the number one women's tennis player in the world.

Riggs, who had won Wimbledon back in 1939 as an amateur at the age of twenty-one, was later (as a professional) the number one male tennis player in the world. He had a reputation for his outrageous sexist claims stating at one time, "Women belong in the bedroom and kitchen, in that order." And another time, "Women play about twenty-five percent as good as men, so they should get about twenty-five percent of the money men get," according to the website History.com.

He fervently believed women's tennis was far inferior to men's tennis. So, at fifty-five years old, he challenged Billie Jean King, twenty-nine, to a match held on September twentieth, 1973, at the Houston Astrodome in Texas. The prize was a winner-take-all $100,000.

Over 30,000 people were in the dome, and I was one of the estimated fifty million who watched worldwide as Billie Jean King triumphed over Riggs. I sat in my own front row, in front of the television, in my small apartment. According to the television program, *60 Minutes*, it was the largest audience to ever watch a tennis match in the United States. It was a landmark moment for women in sports.

Years later in 2017, the event was made into a Hollywood movie, *Battle of the Sexes*, starring Emma Stone as King and Steve Carell as Riggs. You can watch Billie Jean King talk about the match on PBS.

At the time, I was chief photographer of the Wahpeton, North Dakota – Breckenridge, Minnesota *Daily News* and wrote a weekly column. It was my shortest column ever: Billie Jean King, thanks...I needed that! [1]

Defining Moment:

The biggest risk is not taking a risk.

Lesson Learned:

Life is short, it's worth taking risks.

---

[1] That column won first place in the North Dakota Press Women's 1973 annual awards contest for daily newspapers under 20,000 circulation.

CHAPTER 6

Death Lessons

They say such nice things about people at
their funerals that it makes me sad that I'm
going to miss mine by just a few days.

Garrison Keillor

"You know, Barbara," my friend's letter read, "we talked about death once and how I'd never really faced it. You won't believe this, but Dad's death and the subsequent funeral was a positive experience for me. I had the consolation that I'd stepped in when I was needed: Mom was at the end of her rope."

I was living in Germany when I received a letter from my friend in Minnesota. Her letter made me nod with recognition and reflect on the understanding of her newfound strength. I knew exactly what she meant.

I was twelve when I experienced my first lethal, emotional blow. My Dad suffered what used to be called a nervous breakdown. He'd spent time at the nearby state mental hospital In Fergus Falls, where he was subjected to shock treatment therapy. Later people would say he was released from the hospital too early. My father had gone missing for three days before being found a mile down the gravel road in front of our farm. He was hanging in a deserted barn with a rope around his neck.

What traditionally had been joy filled days leading up to Christmas were darkened with our grief. His funeral was held during the day on Christmas Eve, 1957.

Despite experiencing his mother, my grandma's death of natural causes the previous year, I wasn't prepared for the shock of my dad's sudden suicide in an otherwise carefree, happy time living on our Minnesota farm.

It felt as though my childhood was locked in the coffin on that Christmas Eve. I grew up overnight. It was several years before death dropped by again on its causal way–like a forgotten friend.

My grandpa's wife was killed unmercifully in a horrible car accident. She was his second wife, and she was the light of our family. They'd only been married a couple of years. They were so happy. She had him laughing again.

When I heard the news, I was aware that I was becoming hardened to death. It hurt, of course, but I knew life would go on. It always does for those left behind. Eventually, my attitude towards death helped me in my profession as a photojournalist, too.

Along with fun photos I took of people doing interesting things, winning awards, and looking for artistic photos for fillers, as they are called in the newspaper trade, I also had to take photos of horrendous accidents, deadly fires, and other devastating events. However, I was never able to completely divorce myself from the fact that someone's life had been snuffed out.

I'll always remember the only nasty letter I ever received in my five decades of newspaper photography both in the U.S. and Germany. The writer attempted to shame me because I took a photo of a dead seven-year-old boy in the arms of a highway patrolman following a traffic accident. I distinctly remember focusing on the lifeless body in such a way that his injuries and face would not be visible. I focused on the distraught face of the patrolman. My mission was to clearly show – and remind – readers to slow down, be careful, and drive carefully. Unfortunately, the letter writer did not appear to get my message.

Subsequently, the deaths of two grandfathers, a favorite uncle, a twenty-one-year-old brother-in-law, another uncle, three favorite aunts, three cousins, a friend, and a dear friend's father, forced me to learn that death teaches us lessons. You simply must be awake to receive the lesson.

I remember when we lived in Germany, and I belonged to an English discussion group. Each year, the fifteen or so women who attended monthly would choose a moderator. We would discuss and agree on topics for the coming year. The year I was chosen to moderate, I suggested we discuss death. There was a palpable gasp of disagreement. Not one of the women wanted that as a subject to research and talk about. A couple of them had never had a relative or friend who was close to them die, and we were all in our thirties and forties.

After some discussion, I pointed out how important it would be to discuss death. Even if it brought up painful memories, I said to them, it would be a healthy exercise. Finally, I convinced them, and they all begrudgingly agreed.

A few days later I sat down to do some of my research. I started by making a list of all the people who had died in my immediate circle of family and friends. It soon became clear that I had quite a list and had experienced many deaths.

In fact, as it turned out, every two to three years since the age of eleven, someone close to me had died. The deaths that occurred around me happened through natural causes, car and truck accidents, one electrocution, heart attacks, obesity, miscarriages, cancer, and even murder. Family lore told of a distant cousin (whom I didn't know) who was eaten by a shark in the Pacific.

At one point, I began to relate with the well-known political Kennedy clan whose family suffered so many public family tragedies.

"Is there no end to this?" I asked myself.

Of course, there isn't, except for our own death, I came to realize.

But there is a method that can transform the utter despair of death into strength. It's just that sometimes it takes a while to realize that. Like with my dear friend whose father's death became a positive experience for her.

She wrote, "The night before the funeral, everyone else had been there during the day and I got tired of all the commotion at the house. So, I went down to the funeral parlor and just sat with Dad, all alone, for about an hour and a half. I really felt I got from him that evening all the memories and all the strength I needed."

She went on to explain, "I always thought I'd never want an open casket. I'd never want a graveside service. And that coffee at the church afterward was meaningless, until I found out it's not."

Some learn that at forty-five, others at twelve. But whatever age a person's first experience with death is, there is no best time. For me, I am convinced I grew up faster than I would have without those experiences.

Back to our family in the late 1950s. Mother no longer had the luxury of staying home and making fried bread or our evening meals or all the things I'd come to take for granted–like the weekly washing and ironing of our family's clothes.

Luckily, before she married my father, she had completed a course in cosmetology in California and had been employed as a hairdresser. However, she hadn't worked in her field on a salaried basis for the seventeen years she'd lived in Minnesota. She'd always done our neighbors' haircuts and perms, as a nice neighborly thing to do. So, she hadn't lost her touch.

But with three growing daughters–by then thirteen, fifteen, and seventeen–and now a single mother, she knew that she would have to make a living for our family. It was a natural choice to enroll in a course in nearby Fergus Falls to obtain her hairdressing license. But it would take an entire year. The only way it became possible for her to go to school with no income was thanks to my grandpa. Unbeknownst to me, he had owned our farm. I had always assumed –incorrectly–that my parents owned it. After dad's death, he generously "sold" it to my mother. The price? One dollar.

When the auction came in the spring, and we sold our farm, our ponies, all the farm tools and equipment, mother was able to use that money to support us the year she was in beauty school.

At the end of the year, she opened Elva's Beauty Salon in nearby Battle Lake. She would, over the next five years, expand her business to include shops in two other nearby towns. When she knew she wanted to retire, she created a shop in the lower level of our house. Mother was a vastly successful businesswoman.

With Mother at her beauty shop from early morning until late at night, each of us girls had to divide up the household chores and meal preparations. I got "voluntold" to do the ironing. To this day, I hate ironing. Fortunately, today's fabrics often don't require ironing. Suffice it to say that my husband irons his own clothes when they require it.

Death does have a notorious way of disrupting anything resembling the smooth order of life. The ideal way to cope with those changes is to be able to accept them. Unfortunately, unlike death, life isn't that certain.

To be flexible and therefore capable of accepting change is a blessed advantage when dealing with death. I've always admired the way my grandmother was able to sell the home that she had shared with my grandfather for decades. She knew the wisdom of more frugal living and bought a mobile home not far from her friends.

Often without realizing it until much later, death provides us with an inner strength: the realization that life goes on, as it inevitably does. No one can teach another person to accept death– neither their own nor that of a relative or friend. What I learned from death is to accept, change, be flexible, and remain strong.

Death is one of the few unteachable experiences that you must learn for yourself. Once you've learned it, though, chances are, you won't forget it the next time death rips at your guts.

Defining moment:
Death is a learning experience for those left behind.

Lesson Learned:
Being open to change creates new possibilities.

CHAPTER 7

Letters to Mother

Life is not a problem to be solved,
but a reality to be experienced.

Søren Kierkegaard

NOTE: Little did I know that my life would change forever when I boarded a flight to Russia in 1973.

After stops in New York City and Amsterdam, a group of eighty-eight press women from around the U.S. gathered to fly an additional four hours to Moscow. The majority of passengers on the flight were part of our professional group and those four hours generated a lot of excitement and "getting to know you" conversations.

My seatmate, Polly Benn from Arizona, was a fun, chatty woman with a deep voice. Moscow was our first stop on a ten-day trip to the Soviet Union – as it was called then. We had been invited by the Soviet Press Women's Association and had special tours scheduled to historical places; for meetings with Soviet press women; interviews with Russian politicians; and a reception held in our honor. Given this was during the Cold War, it was an extraordinary privilege to be involved with this history-making group.

After settling into our small hotel located across six lanes of bustling traffic from the Kremlin, we attended the National Ballet's performance of Swan Lake. It was absolutely thrilling. It was the first ballet I'd ever seen.

After returning to our hotel, about a dozen of us met at the small bar on the main floor. The others were tired and went to bed. After talking for about half an hour, I noticed an incredibly handsome man in a dark corner of the bar talking to a taller, also good-looking man. Obviously, I neither knew what nationality they were nor if they spoke English, but after noticing that he was also looking me over (perhaps I stood out with my large Fedora hat), I decided to say something. I disengaged from the conversation I was having with my sister travelers, looked him straight in the eye and asked, "Why don't you come over and talk to me?"

Obviously, he understood English, because he left his friend immediately and came walking over and sat across from me. Meeting Ian Purvis that October night was the most magical night of my life. After talking for over an hour and basically closing the bar – all the other press women had gone to bed – we went out walking.

We crossed the scary six-lane street with cars whizzing by in both directions. And there we were: in Red Square! The defensive red brick wall surrounding the Kremlin had to be at least twenty feet tall, impressive in a depressing kind of way. Wow! Lenin's tomb dominated one end with two dull brown military uniformed men guarding it. At the other end of the large square sits the famous St. Basil's Cathedral with its many onion-shaped multicolored domes. It took my breath away. Well, that was probably Ian doing that. We walked Red Square. Then it started to snow lightly. We mischievously taunted the guards, goodness knows why. I think we were both a bit giddy. It's a wonder they didn't arrest us! Anyway, we walked and talked until at least three in the morning at which time we found ourselves at Ian's hotel, a good mile away from my hotel. We had learned from our guide that there would be "Key Ladies" on each floor of our hotels to provide us with our room keys. We were also told that "Nothing gets past them."

Quite like a challenge to test that notion. Ian went up one flight of stairs and I went up another to his room. We made it without being caught! (Or so we thought.) We had stopped for a bottle of Russian sekt (bubbly) which we promptly opened and enjoyed immensely. It didn't take long for us to go from talking to, well, shall we say getting to know each other on a more intimate basis? We were jarred awake a couple of hours later by a shrill telephone ringing. In slow, clear English, albeit with a Russian accent, the voice said, "Your guest must leave NOW."

Holy crap! Busted! We scrambled to get dressed and were out the door in less than five minutes. Ian walked me back to my hotel where I promptly joined Polly in our room. She was fast asleep, of course. And I was, too, as soon as my head hit the feather pillow. Unfortunately, since it was about five a.m. when I got to sleep, I slept through our next agenda item later that morning and missed a tour of the crown jewels! To make a long story short, after seeing each other several times in the following days, both before we left for Leningrad (now back to its original name of Saint Petersburg), we agreed we had something special together and would make plans to see each other again, one way or another.

Two months later, after selling his small sailboat, Ian flew to the U.S. for the first time to spend Christmas with me. It was a terrific week of getting to know each other better, introducing him to my family (they approved), and planning for me to visit him in March 1974 to meet his parents. During that trip, Ian proposed, and we sketched out a plan of action. We needed to determine if he would move to the U.S. or if I would move to England. Oddly enough, as Chief Photographer of the Daily News in Wahpeton-Breckenridge, I was making more money than he was. Plus, I had recently purchased my first brand-new car, a 1974 bright red Plymouth Duster. But in the end, neither of those two facts determined our decision. I shared with Ian that I had a high school dream of living in Europe "someday." After much consideration and many conversations while on my visit to England, we decided that I would give notice at the Daily News and would move to England in a few months. Also, on that trip, I learned that Ian hadn't been truthful about being divorced despite my sharing about my two previous divorces. When he visited at Christmas, he had said he was divorced, too.

In March, I learned that, while he and his wife were separated, they were not divorced. I was devastated. He explained that in England, there is a law that you must be separated for at least two years to obtain a divorce. What kind of crazy law was that?! They hadn't been separated two years. We would learn later, after I had moved to England, that the divorce would not be final until almost a year later in May 1975. Ian made one more trip to see me in June 1974. I was thrilled when he agreed to attend the North Dakota Press Women's annual meeting and awards program in Bismarck, N.D. That year, I won nine first place and two second-place awards for photography, writing, editing, layout, and editorial writing. Ian was able to see and enjoy a bit of the "Wild West" by attending some activities for our group including a rodeo and seeing majestic buffalo for the first time. As it happens, we also got to go horseback riding. I gave my notice to leave in early August. The weeks sped by and soon Mother and Loyd were driving me to Winnipeg where we spent a day visiting the fabulous new Winnipeg Museum and seeing the sights of that beautiful city. The next day, I was beyond excited to fulfill my high school dream of making "someday" a reality on August 10th, 1974. The following four chapters are from letters and postcards to my mother over the next twenty years.

Part I: August 1974 - July 1979

The worst sin you can ever commit to yourself is to
sit and wait for someone to give you money.

Mac Duke

August 10, 1974 - Thanks for driving me to Winnipeg (Manitoba, CAN.). I was excited to arrive in London and spend the rest of my life with Ian. I'll remember it because President (Richard) Nixon resigned two days ago. Big changes are coming.

August 17, 1974 Paris–I went up the Eiffel Tower while Ian was having a delicious French business lunch. Then we're off to Brussels, Holland, and Germany.

September 12, 1974 - *I'd like you all to keep my letters since I may want to use them at some later date.* Friday, I walked into Haverhill –it took half an hour. The next day Ian bought me a 50cc moped for £40 (Worth about $385 today). It goes about 40- 45 mph. It only has 565 miles on it, hasn't been driven for two years, and is a 1971 model. It gets 120 miles to the gallon. A few days later, I took my trusty moped and did the washing at a laundromat in Haverhill. It's about a mile and a half away. I thought it was quite a cheeky sight buzzing along with my bright yellow helmet and a clothes basket piled high on the back of my moped. Last weekend, we drove to

Malden on the coast, about an hour's drive where Ian used to keep the small sailboat he sold to visit me in the U.S. the first time. Malden was gorgeous. We walked around for 6 hours.

October 9, 1974 - [Large postcard from Köln] We're at the Fotokina exhibition, the world's largest trade fair for photography in Cologne. We took the ferry from Dover to Calais because it was too windy for the Hovercraft. It was too rough for the ferry, too, with 20-25-foot waves!

October 30, 1974 - British humor is certainly different. When we're watching television, Ian is roaring with laughter and I'm looking like I just missed the train.

December 17, 1974 - [Postcard of Brussels Town Hall] Brussels is a gorgeous city and much cleaner than Paris. It's loaded with charm.

March 4, 1975 - Ian doesn't come back from Moscow until Wednesday. Then he's off on the 15th for Shanghai and Peking where he'll be for a month. The two weeks in Moscow in January and February in the snow was enough winter for me. I was working nearly the whole time - took less than a roll of slides! The food was lousy, the service was incredibly bad, some people waited three hours for a meal and then didn't get what they ordered.

April 7, 1975 - [Postcard of Warwick Castle] Jeanne (James, our dear neighbor) and I are on a two-day sightseeing visit to Stratford-upon-Avon. We visited Warwick Castle yesterday. Gorgeous. We've seen Shakespeare's birthplace, all rather overwhelming when you stop to think about it.

June 5, 1975 - We got married today in the Canterbury Registry Office. The wedding was very nice, simple, went to St. Giles Church up Church Lane for a blessing, back to the cottage where Mum had laid out a wonderful buffet of crab rolls, salmon sandwiches, shrimp in pastry, fruit salad in a pineapple, and champagne. A friend of Jeanne's surprised us with a lovely decorated small wedding cake. I carried a beautiful Victorian posy that was just perfect. It was all very, very nice. We were both calm and happy. We're leaving tomorrow for our honeymoon in San Antonio de Calonge, Palamós, Spain.

June 24, 1975 - We spent most days on the beach although the water was too cold to go swimming until the day before we left. Our flat was across the beach on the 8th floor. The drive through the French Riviera and Monaco and up through Italy around Lake Garda in the Alps through Austria to Germany was fantastic. We arrived for the Laser exhibition in Munich, Germany right on time.

NOTE: This was not in my letter. The last night at the exhibition in Germany, Ian's boss took us out to dinner. I had a very tasty meal of wiener schnitzel and spätzle and promptly went to the bathroom and threw up. When I got back, evidently, Ian's boss had said, "Looks like she's pregnant!" Given I had an IUD at the time, I hadn't given a thought to getting or being pregnant. Upon return to England, I discovered I was five months pregnant!

August 2, 1975 - Can't call, money is tight. Ian did get a raise this week, but – would you believe – he's still not making what I was earning in Wahpeton. And he must pay his former wife $196 every three months for two years...from the sale of their house. I'm reading a lot about pregnancy and related subjects. I wish I had my Dr. Spock book, but imagine I'll find one here.

August 5, 1975 - Ian's applying for different jobs...one in Holland.

December 6, 1975 - I don't know what Ian sent in the telegram, but in case he missed anything, Andrea La Valleur-Purvis (no middle name) was born at 12:40 p.m. December 3rd, weighs 3.5 kilos (7 lb. 13 oz.) and is 53 centimeters long, (21"). She has light brown hair. Her eyes are dark blue. She looks exactly like Ian, no La Valleur resemblance at all. She's gorgeous, of course!

February 4, 1976 - Andrea's sleeping 12–14.5 hours in the night for the past week, I think that's terrific for only two months! I showed my Russian slides to the Women's Institute today; I miss seeing and reading the U.S. news.

June 14, 1976 - [St. Mary's Church of England, a short walk from our home.] Andrea's christening went off beautifully yesterday.

June 28, 1976 - I'm going with Ian to Paris and Holland in a couple of weeks for a few days. Mum's keeping Andrea.

July 21, 1976 - Made the mistake of drinking hotel tap water in Paris and got terribly ill in both directions.

October 15, 1976 - Andrea started taking her first steps on the 13th, so she was ten months and ten days old.

December 23, 1976 - Ian has just phoned from the office to tell me he got what he wanted, and we will be moving to Germany as soon after March 1st that we can find housing. He's got a terrific deal earning three times his U.K. salary plus extras. We'll also be changing cars to a left-hand drive Ford Estate. We'll be about fifteen miles south of Frankfurt near Darmstadt.

January 19, 1977 - Claire was born so fast Ian didn't even have time to leave the room. I will only stay in the hospital for two days. She is fine. However, she was born with what's referred to as "clicky hips" so she must wear a brace for three months and I won't be able to give her a full immersion bath during that time.

February 18, 1977 - Dropped Andrea off at Mum's but brought Claire along as I'm breastfeeding. Then we drove to Germany to look for a place to live. We found a beautiful flat – on the second floor. The owners, Dieter and Helga Müller, live on the first floor. A single woman lives on the top floor. It's very large and fantastic in Pfungstadt. Post office, shops, doctors, and dentists all within a two minutes' walk. There's a kindergarten school in the next block. It's twenty miles to Ian's job in Höchst in the Odenwald but takes about forty minutes to drive due to winding roads. An interesting thing about renting in Germany: we must supply the entire kitchen and all light fixtures throughout the apartment. Weird.

March 20, 1977 - Sending photos of Claire's christening at St. Mary's Church of England, in Sturmer, Suffolk, the Sunday before we moved to Germany.

March 23, 1977 - Today we are moving to Germany, let the new adventures begin.

April 11, 1977 - Claire got her brace off today. I got another bunch of flowers from Ian yesterday. That's four weeks running now.

June 6th, 1977 - This postcard shows a view of Burg Frankenstein which we can see from our apartment windows. Found out the anniversary card I got for Ian yesterday is a birthday card. Guess I'll have to learn German.

June 2, 1978 - I've started taking Andrea and Claire to a playgroup twice a week on Tuesdays and Thursdays from 9-12:30. I help, so I don't have to pay the equivalent of $8 a morning for both. We have about twenty kids from a few months old to three years. Then they start kindergarten.

August 14, 1978 - Andrea and Claire really like the little Fischer Price characters especially Bert and Ernie. The other day, Andrea asked if Ernie has a penis! We had a trip up the Rhein for 2 hours last week when Ian was on holiday. It was gorgeous.

November 20, 1978 - We're starting to look for a house.

December 9, 1978 - We bought a Grundstück (a piece of land) in the next street from our apartment. I can see it between houses out our kitchen window. Andrea had ten friends for her fourth birthday December 3rd.

January 20, 1979 - Claire had her second birthday yesterday. She's the clown of the family and quite competitive. I suppose it's the La Valleur in her.

March 6, 1979 - Our big news–we got a new color TV. We've been without a TV for a year.

March 16, 1979 - I learned last week that there is a factory in Pfungstadt that makes all the hamburger buns for McDonald's throughout Germany, Belgium, and Holland!! Half a million a day. Plus, they have a small shop that sells their bakery surplus or rejects. It's incredibly cheap. I can buy not only REAL hamburger buns, but BIG MAC BUNS!!!! Ian has built me a shortwave radio from a Heathkit sent from America. I can now listen to BBC radio. They have excellent news, political analysis, fifteen-minute and thirty-minute theaters, and interesting interviews.

April 1979 - Claire won her first race at the annual International Kindergruppe picnic recently. She goes to a playgroup two mornings a week where I've been helping for a year and a half. I am giving that up this month so I can have two mornings to myself. Claire will start kindergarten in September. She's already learned a lot of German from Andrea, so I don't expect much of an adjustment problem for her. It took Andrea six months before she could speak the language. Despite Ian's travels, he's also managed to take up model airplanes seriously this year. He's joined a local club and spends weekends there when he can. I've joined a monthly English Discussion Group which provides a bit of stimulation to the aging brain. We have preset topics which sometimes require research, and the only taboo subject is CHILDREN!! It's particularly interesting because of the variety of countries represented: England, America, Germany, Denmark, Austria, and Czechoslovakia. I also am on the organizational committee of the International Kindergruppe which has various functions throughout the year. So, I was particularly pleased when I got a new VW Polo last month. I seem to spend a third of my time in the car. I'm still attending German class once a week and will continue to do so next year. Our main source of entertainment is having friends over and me cooking using my Cordon Bleu Cookery Books.

April 17, 1979 - On our trip to northern Italy two weeks ago, Ian and I spent two nights in Arona on Lake Maggiore and then drove by Milan and up to Lake Como to a small village north of Lecco (which should be on the map). We spent the entire Saturday afternoon with a guy who was speaking Italian, German and French and was trying to locate ancestors from Ian's great-grandfather (b. 1848) who had emigrated as a lad from Italy to England in 1860. The group of young boys and a priest came to learn the furniture-making trade. We went with this guy to the church and the Records office, but that was closed as it was the weekend. Then we went to the cemetery which was busy *with life*! No joke. There were people cleaning, putting flowers on graves, having animated conversations, and praying. The best part of it was all the graves have photographs on the stones, even the ones from the late 1880s. We saw lots of people with the same last name, but we don't know if they were related. I would highly recommend people visiting Italy to go to some old cemeteries where they may have the same experience. In any case, it's fascinating to see photographs on gravestones going back a hundred years.

June 5, 1979 - Our fourth wedding anniversary! We're sitting beside Lake Lucerne in Switzerland having a cup of coffee. Before leaving yesterday, we spent four hours in a notary office signing papers for our Grundstück. Prices for houses are about DM 165 per square meter. We've bought a house, well, the land and the structure that needs to be built. It's in the next street to ours. It's a double house half the literal translation, it's a duplex. We hope to move in next year between February and May. It's not what we had hoped to get, but it's in Pfungstadt and that's where we want to be. It's also $35,000 cheaper than the one-family houses we've been looking at. I bought a three-speed bike for $185. I thought I'd like something special and it's great fun. I've got a basket for my shopping on the back and a seat for Claire on the front. Andrea does quite well on her bike. I expect the training wheels will come off soon.

June 11, 1979 - I learned that Pfungstadt has the most expensive swimming pool in Germany with a built-in wave machine, would you believe?! It's quite fun.

June 14, 1979 - [Postcard of Pilatus aerial cable car with view of Lake Lucerne, Rigi and Bürgenstock] It was great to have Ian's mum visit us so she could join us on our trip to Switzerland. Mum and I went to Pilatus on her birthday on this cable car. It was fantastic.

Part II: August 1979 - July 1984

You must be the change you wish to see in the world.

Gandhi

NOTE: Ian quit his job and started his own company. That was the beginning of fifteen years of cash flow problems and desperate financial woes. Still, the girls were growing, taking music lessons, starting kindergarten, then school, and joining Girl Scouts at the American Base in Darmstadt. I had a photo printed in a Paris newspaper. We lived through several months of Mum's illness with a malignant brain tumor during which time I drove to England to care for her for a week.

August 28, 1979 - We returned from England last night. The trip takes about seven hours from our place to England, then 40 minutes on the Hovercraft and another 35 minutes from Ramsgate to Ian's parents in Kingston, a quaint village outside of Canterbury, Kent.

September 28, 1979 - Andrea and Claire start music lessons in a couple of weeks. It is a group of three and four-year-olds who will have an hour a week learning rhythm, a few simple songs, and percussion—cymbals, triangles, etc. My friend, Beth Fagg, a musician, is their teacher. She's charging one dollar each for each child for the hour. I thought that was very reasonable. I started a German class last Thursday evening. It was supposed to be for intermediate students, but in fact, it is a beginning group. It consists of four Polish people who've only been in the country a month and don't speak any German; a mother and daughter from Naples, Italy; a woman from the West Bank near Jerusalem; a woman from Spain;

my American neighbor from Des Moines, Iowa; a sixteen-year-old au pair from French-speaking Switzerland and me. I dare say, I speak the best which, of course, isn't saying much! On Tuesday, the fall meetings of our English Discussion Group started. There were ten women, five of whom were newcomers. There were six women from England, including myself, others from Austria, Germany, and Vietnam. My Danish friend was unable to attend.

October 25, 1979 - Ian is very dissatisfied with his company (Ealing Beck) so he will possibly be changing jobs next year. The building construction for our house hasn't started yet. It's very expensive.

December 1, 1979 - I'll be baking two birthday cakes tomorrow. One for Andrea's kindergarten and one for her party. It should be fun. Ten children (three Deutsche), all three years old except Andrea will be four. We've got games, contests and a puppet theater planned.

January 14, 1980 - Anniversary card–getting ready to go into the hospital with Andrea for her ear operation.

February 4, 1980 - I was so nervous about Ian giving his notice at Ealing Beck, that I broke out in hives. He's been with Ealing Beck for eleven years. I told the women in our English Discussion Group about ice fishing in Minnesota and they couldn't comprehend it. Mother, please take photos of Loyd's ice fishing house, the ice saw, the hole, etc. so I can share with my friends. We're going up the street to the Evangelische (Lutheran) Kindergarten for Bastle Nachmittag (craft afternoon). I went there to see if I could get the girls into a class. Claire came out with another doozy last week. I was getting dressed one morning and putting my bra on when Andrea said, "When I was little, I had my food out of there [pointing to my left breast] and my drink out of here," [pointing to my right breast] she said poking me. Claire, in her three-year-old wisdom, thought for about thirty seconds and said, "That's because we didn't have a table!"

February 23, 1980 - I have decided to make a cathedral window patchwork quilt. It may take five to ten years to do, but I want to do it. It will keep me busy when I'm with Andrea at all her ear doctor appointments. It doesn't require a quilting frame.

February 29, 1980 - They dug the Keller (cellar) Monday. All is going well with Anaspec. In fact, Ian received his first order yesterday over the phone for DM 25,000. It's exciting. His office won't be ready until April 1st, but it doesn't matter.

March 6, 1980 - I went to Nuremberg with Ian. I went to the Spielzeug [Toy] Museum while he was at a business meeting.

April 17, 1980 - Started Anaspec Electro Optics GmBH on April 1st. We celebrated in England. Ian's partner, Bill, had a party for us. We came back from England to find the cellar walls of our house up and by the end of the week, they had the inside walls up, too. Today they're starting on the downstairs/main floor, or the first floor as it's called in Germany. At this rate–and with good weather–they'll have the Raubau (basically the frame of the house with a roof) done in no time.

May 10, 1980 - The Thursday before Easter I had my first photo gig since leaving Wahpeton. I took photos of an artist while another journalist, Gale Wiley, interviewed him. It should be in the World Herald Tribune published in Paris this week. Exciting!

June 4, 1980 - They poured the last concrete steps for the top floor yesterday. They now are doing the inside walls to the top (third) floor, then the side walls with the roof which will be on soon. Ian has been very busy and had orders for over a quarter of a million DM in his first two months of business! BUT, although he has orders, they won't be delivered until July, so that means it's a bit tight for about six weeks.

July 5, 1980 - I'm setting up a darkroom at Ian's office. At the house in Pfungstadt, they have started putting in the heating and water pipes. I'm in charge of the English Discussion Group this year. We've set the topics. All sound interesting–most were my ideas. They even agreed to talk about death although at first, no one wanted to tackle that subject. I convinced them since we all must face it sometime or other, it would be smart to talk about it before it becomes a crisis in our lives.

August 18, 1980 - A, C, and Jennifer (my niece) stayed with Mum while Ian and I drove to Devon. Yesterday A, C, and Jennifer sang "Jesus Loves Me" for the family church service. It was a hoot! Claire starts kindergarten in two weeks.

September 2, 1980 - Claire started kindergarten yesterday. Andrea started English lessons yesterday, for two hours a week through the Kindergruppe which has seven to eight children. Today it's music lessons at Beth's. The wiring and sanitation work is finished on the house. The windows are being done. Sunday, I start teaching Sunday School at the American base in Darmstadt. I don't know why I volunteered. I feel quite inadequate. I do know I have a well-balanced idea of values though and hope I can do alright. I'll have third-graders, eight and nine-year-olds. Ian thinks I'm bonkers.

September 8, 1980 - Just bought our tickets, we leave here November 17th via Chicago, arrive Minneapolis at 6:45 p.m. Ian will fly back via Montreal on November 30th; we'll come back together on December 8th. The darkroom is set up. I'm glad to say I haven't lost my touch. The photo of the girls walking up Church Lane will remain one of my all-time favorites. It is taken as a "tribute" to my favorite photographer, W. Eugene Smith who worked as a Life magazine photographer. Yesterday was six years to the day that I moved to England. I'm in the middle of baking bread.

September 26, 1980 - Written on Anaspec stationary Pallaswiesenstraße 63, 6100 Darmstadt. I'm at the office, Ian has his first ad in a technical journal that came out this week, so I thought I'd come in and hopefully answer all the inquiries. I've had one for DM 10,000 so that's been worth it. And in the post this morning, he had another inquiry. His bank balance yesterday was DM 45,000!!! Was pleased that Sharon will have a birthday party for Andrea. I'll make the cake, I enjoy that.

October 12, 1980 - Ian and I got away for a couple of days to the Titisee and Baden Baden. They've started plastering the walls of our house.

November 5, 1980 - Dreadful weather, cold, hope radiators come next week so we can get the heating on. They poured our flooring this week and it has little bubbles all over, not good. The girls and I (not sure about Ian) will be there soon. I'll sleep in the trailer; it'd be better for the girls to sleep in the spare bedroom.

February 7, 1981 - Moved into our new house.

March 18, 1981 - Your letter about Joe [Kotnik, my first ex-husband] was extremely distressing. Not only because I have been low lately. But, although I've had no feelings for him for nearly fifteen years, I did spend three years of my life with him. What bothers me is that it was in Everett, Washington that he chose to end his life. And it was such a horrid death. I can't imagine him dousing himself with gasoline at a gas station and lighting himself on fire. He spent three awful days in the hospital before he died. It was on the national news. I don't know if I ever told you, but the January after we were divorced, he phoned and begged me to come back to him, he cried for more than half an hour. I was living in Everett at the time. I've written to his parents and asked a few questions and said the matter of his pension should be dealt with through a lawyer. I did not say anything about how I feel–which is this: I would not reject the $5,000 he left to me as the recipient of his life insurance policy. I believe he wanted to repay me for:

1) The $1,500 inheritance I got from Grandpa La Valleur, of which I saw not one cent because it was spent on suits for Joe to teach and pay off one of his loans.

2) The year I worked to put him through his final year of college, he had promised me that I could go back to college when he got a job. That, if you recall, I tried to do at the University of Minnesota, Morris. But after one month, I was forced to quit so that I could be at home to make his midday meal–which he could have bought for twenty cents at Starbuck High School.

So, I suppose I would say the "debt" would be his way of repaying me. And perhaps he thought that, too. I don't know. But there must have been a reason that he had not changed his pension given he had been married and had two children. He had plenty of time to change it. I do not want to make an ordeal about it. I'm sure his parents, Cress and Jibs, will be very surprised that I feel this way. But I do.

April 7, 1981 - I have been out "pounding the pavement" looking for jobs of any kind–developing film, secretarial at ESOC, a photo shop owned by an American. Andrea lost her first tooth Sunday with another loose one on the bottom. The drive to England wasn't bad. It took five and a half hours to drive to Calais, one and a half hours on the ferry to Dover and then only ten minutes to Kingston. I got a letter from Cress and the next day, one from the state Teachers Retirement Assoc. The money involved is $4,000. Quite frankly, I think I'm entitled to it. He'd been divorced for four years. I spent all that money on him from Grandpa and in part because of him, it took me nine years to finish my four-year college degree.

May 6, 1981 - I started a part-time job, two hours a day doing darkroom work in an ad agency called Pool Gesellschaft für Werbefotografie GmbH, Pool for short. My boss, Ramon Schischte, is very nice; I develop film and make 5 x 7 prints of advertising products; hope to make DM 400-500 a month to help with housekeeping money. It will be three months tomorrow that we moved into our house, there are still things by the builder that have not been finished. We've only seen him once since we moved in. Andrea must have that same ear operation again on May 18th, fluid in the middle ear.

June 8, 1981 - My boss reminds me of Columbo, so now I call him Ramon-do. With part of my first month's salary, I ordered bits and pieces for the main bathroom–towel holders, toilet paper holder, soap dishes and opened a savings account. My nerves are shot. Ian's too, but I'm worse. This self-employed business is a heck of a lot more work than anything I'd ever imagined. Beth and Steve are moving back to England next month so the girls' music lessons will end.

June 29, 1981 - Ian and I are on a one-day away fling to Strasbourg, two hours from home. The kids are with friends.

August 26, 1981 - Yesterday we got a very big order, DM 65,000!!!! The month of August he got DM 125,000 worth of orders, which is more than the months from January through August! [My cousin] Pam and Kirk Vogen who live near Dallas, Texas, came for a visit; he was working in Frankfurt.

October 20, 1981 - They're starting our Verputz, ie. stucco, on Monday.

November 24, 1981 - Two weeks ago today we had a bad experience. Andrea was bitten by a big black dog when we were at my friend, Cheryl Kreutzer (now Johnstone) for coffee while Claire was at her English class. The bite was right on her top lip. It was extremely deep, nearly through, in fact. I drove frantically the whole way while my friend, who is thankfully a nurse, held her lip closed to stop the profuse bleeding. I didn't realize it until I arrived at the ER a mile away that I had on my emergency brake the whole time. Andrea had to have six stitches, even though the doctor was apprehensive about stitching it up. He said normally, a dog bite shouldn't be sewn, but because it was so deep and so bad, he had to. Luckily there was no infection and has, in fact, healed quite well. The whole experience was just horrible, and it was worse than having a baby for me! I was a nervous wreck for about three days. Andrea had to have a big injection of Valium to quieten her then she was good as gold. She didn't cry when she was being sewn up and had to go back every day for a week and she never once complained. She hadn't provoked the dog. She had knelt and put her nose up to his nose and *chomp*!!

December 9, 1981 - Ian has grown a mustache. He looks like a Polish solidarity leader now. Or perhaps an Italian Pizza Shop owner. The house is finally done on the outside.

April 2, 1982 - I asked for a raise, I'm only making DM10 an hour. Andrea has had earaches again.

April 13, 1982 - This is a difficult letter to write, but I don't know what else to do. We are in a very delicate and dangerous way financially and I want to know if you can help us? Ian's business is going, but the big problem is with customers who don't pay after receiving their orders. The company is badly overdrawn, over his bank guarantee at the limit, which is illegal. In fact, Ian could go to jail for it technically. In Germany, like most places, you must have money to borrow money, ludicrous. Ian has several orders, but he can't make any more equipment because he can't buy the supplies he needs until he is paid for delivered orders. There are still a few other companies who owe him thousands! So, I'm asking if you could loan us $2,500 for what period, I don't know. But at least we could live for a couple of months while this gets sorted out! We are both extremely nervous. Still, I am confident things will get better. I would hate to see his company go bankrupt, but it may come to that. If you haven't got it, I will understand. I told Ian I was writing this letter and he said nothing. It hurts to swallow your pride. But I believe in what he's doing. I know it will work.

May 24, 1982 - Prepare yourself - letter of gloom! Mum was rushed to the hospital last week after collapsing minutes before Dad was supposed to go to work. She's in a neurological hospital in south London. She has been diagnosed with an inoperable brain tumor. They are not hopeful. She has lost the use of her right arm. Uncle Bill has had a bad case of shingles. Andrea fell on a nail at

Ringenwald's and had a 4" cut requiring 7 stitches. Claire fell on her bike and had to have her lip sewn up last week. She asked me why *I* couldn't sew up her lip.

June 3, 1982 - Mum's at home. Her bed was moved downstairs to the living room.

June 11, 1982 - Proud of you for opening E+ with Eivor. A Scandinavian gift shop in the old Camp Roma store will be a great addition to that resort area.

June 12, 1982 - Mum is deteriorating fast, she can no longer talk & is not aware.

June 22, 1982 - Writing from England as I left the girls with Ian for a week, so I could help care for Mum.

July 10, 1982 - Postcard from Weggis, Switzerland, near Küßnacht. We are renting a sailboat tomorrow for the day. That should be a fun treat and help us to relax. I've never done that.

August 3, 1982 - It was Andrea's first day at school today and quite an event. She had on the new dress that I made, her new school satchel and a big "Zuckertüte" which is a cone supposedly filled with sweets, but I put two sweets and the rest more practical things like a skirt and blouse I had made, a pen, hair clips, socks & school supplies. I took lots of pictures of her and her friend across the street, Nina Hilz. They are in the same class so that will be convenient. Ian even came home to go with us on her first day. I was very pleased. Not all fathers can do that, but an awful lot of them were there. Nina's dad took the morning off. Claire was impossible all day because Andrea got so much attention. I tried to tell her that her turn was coming soon, but that didn't help today. I think June and Randy should get a divorce. She would find life a lot easier without the constant friction. Sad, but true.

August 17, 1982 - Mum died today. I'm also sad that our British friends, Mary & Alan Lowe, are moving back to England on October 1st. Nina's mother, Roswitha, is giving me German lessons; in return I do odd sewing and mending jobs for her. Claire is such a fussy eater.

October 13, 1982 - I started writing the dates in the German style with the day before the month and year. I'm thinking and even dreaming in German. Ian's partner Bill Vince's business in England was closed by the bank. Unfortunately, he had provided a bank guarantee for Ian. Sometimes I wonder if being self-employed is all it's cracked up to be. Ian works so hard all the time. His business is doing alright, and he will finally catch up at the end of the year and make a small profit. But what a struggle! I can't work in the office much because it's too complicated and the German is all technical. I brought my darkroom home from Ian's office where I never had the time to use it & put it up with all my other junk upstairs. Have printed three times this week.

October 23, 1982 - A most astounding coincidence took place yesterday. As I was looking at the house of Andrea's friend, Nadine Ringenwald, with her mother Christiana, I saw the picture of the lovely, young girl that you have in your living room. If I remember correctly, we were told that it was painted by Loyd's Aunt. It is the exact *same* picture only it looks like a photo of a painting. So that family tale is debunked. Christina said the woman's name is Duchess Pototzky and she is supposed to be a relative of hers! One wonders how those family rumors start. Would you please look to see if there is a name on the back of the frame? Or take it out of the frame and look to see if there is anything written behind it? Please take a color photo of the painting and send it to me a.s.a.p. I want to show Christiana. Small world, eh?

October 25, 1982 - What's this about June applying to med. school? Our English Discussion Group topic this month is Test Tube Babies. Should be interesting. I have a shooting pain up my back, worse than labor...lumbago. I am very depressed, cry a lot, and am generally miserable.

December 9, 1982 - Dad bought the girls black patent leather shoes with a strap. I sent him drawings of their feet & shoes. They don't sell that style of girls' shoes in Germany. He's going to Heather's for Christmas. We went to a dinner dance Saturday night in Frankfurt and danced until 3 a.m. The girls stayed with Peter & Josie, an American couple who live in our old apartment. It was great fun. My whole body ached on Sunday. I made two Stollens today. Last week I bought A & C their walking talking dolls, 60 cm tall. Now I can sew doll clothes! Claire asked me if you could get her another tomato pillow cover just like the one you got before. I had made a matching one for her doll. I've re-created the flat pillow twice, but she liked her tomato! Must go now and take Andrea to her boyfriend's house! He came yesterday–1st ever visit of this type– and they sat watching tv, his arm around her. But I'm happy to report that when Andrea kissed him on the cheek, he moved to another chair.

February 8, 1983 - We've all been sick. Now Claire's got Scarlet Fever. I made her a shiny red devil costume complete with a cap with horns for Fasching. Her tongue is the same color of bright red!

March 3rd, 1983 - The girls and I will be driving to England for 10 days in April.

March 13, 1983 - I'm at the ear, nose, throat doctor in Darmstadt with a waiting room full of people. I'm here because my snoring has gotten worse in the last few months, and I've started waking Ian up every night and he can't get back to sleep. He is in England for the week. He was supposed to come home tomorrow, but his father rang, and Dad's mother died yesterday. She was 93 and had been senile for the last four years, so it was not unexpected. She lived in a home in Exeter near Ian's Aunt Ann & Uncle Bill. I've booked us to fly to the states July 1st. I want to have the 4th & 7th with you. My 20th class reunion will either be the 2nd or the 9th–we'll also go to CA July 20-26th. I want the girls to see Grandma Jo & Aunt Al & all the cousins & go to Disneyland. They're just the right age and they'll love it. The flight will cost us a fortune: DM 6,500!! Last week, the girls earned a Girl Scout patch by selling 32 boxes of cookies together to neighbors and teachers. I must make their uniforms. Ian's leasing a new car for me this week, a VW Variant Passat, a station wagon. Last week I had a call from my friend in Braunschweig, Florian Sosnitza. Claire is a good little helper in the garden, but Andrea just wants to play.

April 20, 1983 - Happy Birthday, Mother! We had a cabin for the night crossing from Ostend to Felixstowe. It was a very rough crossing, the next night a Hovercraft crashed into the jetty, and people were killed due to Force 10 winds! We stayed with Ian's cousins Meg & Roger Baker, then drove to Devon to stay with Ann & Bill. I just love the Devon countryside. The huge, rolling hills with so many stone walls, built hundreds of years ago & the architecture is so different with many thatched cottages. We had a walk on the Moors and saw the wild ponies. Then we drove up through the Cotswold's to Heather's and John's before driving to Felixstowe. No news from Dad. I haven't talked to him for eight months. His own brother and sister can't understand this new relationship with his housekeeper either. They're not impressed with Maureen. That's being kind. Not sure if it's to do with the fact that she's Ian's age.

June 9, 1983 - June flew to Hannover and Florian took her to the former East Germany. Unfortunately, she had her billfold stolen.

June 19, 1983 - June and I went to Switzerland for 3 days with NO KIDS!

July 31, 1983 - Thanks for all you did for us on our trip to Minnesota. The girls will remember it for a long time. Cousin Roy (Ontiveros) took them to Disneyland.

August 23, 1983 - We've had another two weeks of *very tight* living. In fact, I didn't even have any money for stamps. And they cut off our phone for not paying the bill. It makes me wish–almost–that I'd never gone to the states. That entire trip cost us DM 9,000.

September 6, 1983 - After returning from a visit to the U.S.–This is the first time since leaving the states that I had an adjustment problem when coming back from a holiday. Although it was nice to be home in Germany, it's so much more stressful living here. In the states, people are more relaxed and laugh more. Ian has been much, much better, but he could still be nicer to me. I have decided just to leave the room if he speaks in a hateful, condescending voice. We had a letter about someone taking us to court for not paying a bill. Ian is paying it this week. But we've had absolutely no money since we came back. The refrigerator is always bare, and we are living from day to day. And I keep thinking, if we hadn't spent that money going to the states, we'd be all right and I wouldn't be so damn depressed.

September 12, 1983 - Had a good talk with Ian Friday night. Told him I am not happy & need something from him besides dirty clothes to wash & a quick roll in the hay. He claims he is totally exhausted when he comes home from work & just simply switches off. It doesn't look like he'll change soon. I'm trying to accept it & not get depressed. Everyone has problems. I know. Mine are no better or worse than yours or anyone's.

September 19, 1983 - I'm selling some of the cross-stitch items I'm making, decorations, and nameplates for kid's rooms. I had a German Tupperware party last week with 12 women from five different countries. They bought almost DM 1,000 worth. I get 5 "presents" as a result, a bathroom scale, a shopping bag, clothes brush. The woman who did it said she'd never in 10 years had such an interesting group. We're not going to England during the girls' fall break, can't afford it.

October 11, 1983 - It'll be the 10th anniversary on the 16th of meeting Ian in Moscow. I'm busy with Scouts, 10-15 hours a week.

November 2, 1983 - I'm doing a trade with my hairdresser; I'm helping her 10-year-old with English lessons, and I get my hair done every week.

December 7, 1983 - Claire got chickenpox Saturday–½ hour before Andrea's birthday party! Bill & Ann are coming on the 21st.

December 30, 1983 - On the brighter side, life seems to be turning "up" financially. Ian more than doubled his turnover of 1982 and already has orders into April 1984. He bought us a microwave when he went to England. They are just now starting to come on the German market. The girls have both had chickenpox now.

January 5, 1984 - The girls are fine now. Andrea's chickenpox marks are gone. I hope to visit England in February during the winter school break. I must meet this girlfriend of Dad's. She's still married but has left her husband of 20 years and moved in with Dad! I have got a lot of aches & pains with arthritis.

February 9, 1984 - Planning our fall trip to England in October during the girls' school break. The situation in England is rather unfortunate. Dad & Heather aren't talking. I'm going with the girls to England at Easter. Bill and Ian have gone skiing the past three years, but I've never gone. I don't know how to ski, and I don't have any equipment. The girls enjoy Scouts. They will be selling Girl Scout cookies again soon. Each one must sell 48 boxes. I'm having them all here this month–15 girls ages 6 - 9, four speak German, one other is British, besides Andrea & Claire, two are Black or as A & C say, 'brown' and one is Chicano.

February 23, 1984 - Maureen has a 16-years-old son. Her daughter, 21,Lowe is married. Dad is over the moon. She, no doubt, is as well. He wants to get married asap, but the divorce has only just been started. I haven't met her yet, but Ian says she's very meek & timid & that I probably wouldn't find her too interesting. She's never been further than Dover.

March 10, 1984 - enjoying Brownies & being co-leader of the troop. My Brownie name is "Brown Owl."

April 18, 1984 - Heather, Jennifer, James, Andrea, Claire & I are on a London double-decker bus having a tour of the city.

April 30, 1984 - I was never so glad to be home after a trip to England. We had a super time for the first week. But the time at Dad's was just awful. It'll be a long time before I go back there.

Without going into detail, Maureen has taken over *everything*. She - with Dad's permission - has taken all the things Mum made off the walls. That I can understand. Plus, she's put away (for Heather & I to go through) all the other things of Mum's—except the very nice things. I'm not being catty. It's true. Dad has told her that it's *her* house & everything in it is *hers.* Even things done by his Grandchildren were taken down. Plus, all the photos that were in a box - including those recent ones of the four grandchildren were nowhere to be seen. She didn't allow us one minute alone with Granddad. We have always gone to the pub for a drink b/4 lunch. We have always gone out for an afternoon together to talk, either to the beach or shopping. He's always been full of fun and jokes with me as well as being affectionate. Well, that is obviously over. Ian was very upset. Lord knows I was, too. I was so nervous I couldn't eat the last day and got dreadful diarrhea. They left me on my own several times and ignored me as well. I couldn't believe it was so awful. Dad didn't take the girls for a walk with Max - what used to be the highlight of their trip - and he didn't read one goodnight story to them. So that is the situation. You can forget about going there in October. She is only 39 & still married. He's 65. He seems happy, but he was also very nervous while were we there. I couldn't talk to him directly about anything. Every conversation had to go through Maureen.

June 12, 1984 - I haven't got enough money to pay for a stamp for this letter. It's not because the business isn't going well. Ian has shipped over DM 100,000 of goods recently, but people haven't paid him, and he's got orders for more than DM 100,000. So, the business is okay. But the cash flow is dreadful.

June 18, 1984 - We had our 9th anniversary on June 5th. It's 10:45 a.m. and I'm sitting on the terrace under the umbrella. I've already been to the gynecologist, Ian's office and delivered two tables to a transport company at Frankfurt airport. Saturday, we went to a gorgeous hotel, practically a palace, built by Queen Victoria's daughter, Victoria, to celebrate Queen Elizabeth's official birthday - a function of the 64 Club from Frankfurt. Most people were English.

July 28, 1984 - Dad & Maureen are getting married on August 10th. He retires this week after 50 years with the same company. He had a real quarrel over the phone with Heather, so she won't go to the wedding. We won't either, not that we were invited.

July 30, 1984 - I had to drive to Scotland with the girls and Sigrid, our neighbor girl, without Ian–1,400 km (ca. 900 miles) Ian is flying over to join us tomorrow. There are seals in the lochs (lakes) 10 min.'s walk through a pasture. I love Scotland. It's my favorite European country.

Part III: August 1984 - July 1989

To write about a place, you must live there.

Jonathan Ames

NOTE: *During this five-year period, we discovered the gorgeous town of Bensheim and longed to move there despite all the work and expenses of building our new house. We successfully found the perfect older house with a very large backyard, almost unheard of in Germany where three generations often live together in the same house on a tiny lot. Family visits and trips and more cash flow problems are reoccurring themes. A highlight was me learning to ski in the Alps at 40!*

August 28, 1984 - Bill, Ian's uncle, had a stroke last week and now has pneumonia. He's more like a father to Ian.

September 24, 1984 - The exchange rate is DM 3.03 = $1; could you bring wild rice, playing cards–German cards are different; Cheerios for Claire. Dad has four grandchildren whom he seems to have forgotten. He doesn't call & when he does, never asks about them. If only he'd chosen a nice, normal woman instead of someone who is jealous & has no confidence.

December 12, 1984 - I wrote about having large pencil-sized veins in each leg. I need to go to the hospital to have them stripped in February.

December 27, 1984 - Girls wrote thank you letters for Christmas dolls, Andrea's is named Timothy and Claire's is Evi.

February 4, 1985 - Sewing projects–curtains, kitchen stool covers, oven mitts, and toaster cover. Ian is usually up and out by 7, sometimes earlier.

February 18, 1985 - Had right leg vein stripped; nothing to the left leg, no pain there; Andrea had a sledding accident, using Claire's sled she ran into a tree on the Todesbahn (Deadly Hill) in the woods by Pfungstadt; had to go to ER, took her friend 45 min. to pull her home on a sled; nothing broken, just badly bruised, bloody, and swollen. We paid about DM 1,000 for my Singer sewing machine 7 years ago!

March 25, 1985 - Claire had her 6th tooth pulled. If I had it to do over again, I would have bought a horrible dummy (pacifier) rather than have all this dental work later! English Discussion group theme tonight was on consumerism; we sound like a group of jet setters–2 women were off skiing in Switzerland, one in Japan, one in South America, one in Australia for 6 weeks, one couple had gone to England. There were 4 new women, one each Canadian, German, South African, and Australian.

May 20, 1985 - If only we could move to Bensheim.

June 12, 1985 - Planning to go into hospital to have my tubes tied.

July 13, 1985 - On holiday at Starnberger See south of Munich, rented a holiday apartment from Frau Glas, a weaver, and Herr Glas in Possenhofen, a village near the Starnberger See. Very artistic area, DM 55 a night ($17), he makes wooden doll furniture without using nails, expensive; I bought two doll chairs for A's & C's dolls.

August 7, 1985 - Getting ready to move from Pfungstadt to Bensheim. It's very hectic with boxes all over the place. We're moving ourselves, of course, because it saves several hundred marks. Although I'm taking my kitchen with, it's going to cost over $1,000 – yes, that's dollars! – to make it fit with a few new cupboards, countertops etc. Claire's feather collection is now over 400! Andrea has a new full-sized bike. Our Brownie Troop 424 was at the opening of the new McDonald's Drive-In in Darmstadt. The group of Boy & Girls Scouts could eat all they wanted for free.

August 19, 1985 - We sold our house in Pfungstadt for DM 355,000!

August 28, 1985 - We're still in Pfungstadt, living among boxes, empty walls, and confusion. The paperwork on our house in Bensheim has been totally fouled up and I have no idea when we'll move. The children must be taken every day to school which starts at 7:55 a.m. and today, Andrea gets out at 11:20 while Claire has school until 1:05! We've had to get an incredible number of official documents. One is called an unbedenktlichkeitbescheinigung. That's one word. I really don't think you - or any Americans - can imagine how difficult life can be in a foreign country. In America, things are so easy. The standard is so high, people don't tolerate red tape – they expect it here. What frustrates me, is that I have no control over the situation. I have no power. It's dreadful.

September 6, 1985 - Moved to Bensheim.

September 20, 1985 - Today a neighbor just "popped" in for tea– uninvited–formally, that is. I feel like I have arrived! It's such a seldom occasion. Roswitha, in 4 years, never once did that. Holland is just great except someone broke into Ian's car & stole his radio/tape player worth DM 1,200! He had parked for ca. ½ hr. to pick me up at the train in front of the Holiday Inn. All covered by our insurance, thankfully. Girls don't have English in school yet, it starts in their 5th year. Andrea is in Pfadfinders (German Scouts), but as it's for older boys and girls, Claire isn't eligible yet. Andrea & I planted 835 crocuses in the grass of our yard–I plan to go with the girls to England during Easter vacation next year and visit Ian's cousins, Meg & Roger. Then we'll drive to Heather's, visiting Jeanne James on the way and Mary Lowe.

October 7, 1985 - Andrea was really thrilled with the quilt you sent, Mother. Of course, Claire is terribly jealous because she hasn't got hers yet. Claire always expects to get everything that Andrea gets. She seems to forget she's a year younger.

October 15, 1985 - Just got back from a meeting at the Hemsberg Schule at which I was chosen the "Ausländische Vorsitzende" (foreigner representative) to the equivalent of the PTA. There are about 360 students. The international students include 8 Italians; 6 Turkish; 7 Spanish; 2 Persian; 2 British/American; 2 Yugoslavian; 1 French and 1 Canadian. A woman rang me tonight to invite me tomorrow to see how their family harvest grapes for wine. Her daughter is in Claire's class. Andrea has passed her bike test, written & practical, so she'll get her bike license soon. Children in the 4th grade must take the test in school. They go to a special place with bikes from the police & AAA (in Germany, ADAC). Once they pass the test, they can officially ride their bikes to school. But it's only 5 minutes to walk so I won't let them take their bikes to school. Besides which, there aren't enough bike parking places. Claire had her ears pierced last week. Now they both have them done.

October 31, 1985 - I started Ti Chi Chuan classes.

December 8, 1985 - Ian left on Friday for 10 days in England. He always seems to go away in December. He rang today & someone broke into his car again trying to get the tv he uses for testing his equipment, but it was too big, and they couldn't get it out of the hole in the back window that they broke. The life-like baby dolls arrived & they're super.

January 11, 1986 - The Mount House East Wing in Braisted near Seven Oaks where we will stay when you and Sharon come is about an hour from London. B&Bs are too expensive & you must be out by 10 a.m. It's £120 for the week plus £25 extra if we want central heating. It has two fireplaces & a wood-burning stove. I enjoyed the visit from Kaye & Allan Braaten from Wahpeton and Betty & Ray Kummer from Colfax. Both Kaye & Ray are on the Richland County Commission which I used to cover when I was Chief Photographer at the Daily News. The decision as to what kind of school the girls go to will be made soon. Andrea's grades have fallen since Pfungstadt. Unlike Claire, the first two months for Andrea were hard. I've thought of something you can bring when you come: Bisquick & Nacho flavored Dorito Chips! Only 46 days until you & Sharon are here!

February 5, 1986 - I weigh 65 kilos (143.3 lbs.). We meet with teachers in a couple of weeks to decide where Andrea will go to school next year. We'll explain the three types of schools when you get here.

February 21, 1986 - Can you please bring one Jolly Time Buttery Seasoning for popcorn?

April 7, 1986 - Sunday we left to drive to northern Germany to pick up our puppy, Duke, a liver Belton colored English Setter. He seems to fit in nicely. 700 km (435 mi) there & back.

May 14, 1986 - June called to tell me about Monte dying. Ian came back from a trip and gave me a pair of lovely pearl earrings "for working so hard" while he was gone. They have 3 tiny pearls with a small ruby in the middle.

June 9, 1986 - I'm looking forward to the end of the school year. We are going to Scotland from July 12th to August 2nd.

July 2, 1986 - I really treated myself. Instead of putting my DM 410 paycheck in the bank, I went out & spent every pfennig on clothes for ME! A summer dress, skirt, three tops, nightie & sandals. It was fun.

July 21, 1986 - We had an accident and smashed our new Volvo today. No one was hurt. We were coming back from Glasgow where we'd dropped A/C at the plane to fly to London. There, Heather picked them up and took them along with Jennifer & James and put them on a train to Cornwall for a week at a kids' adventure camp.

August 6, 1986 - What a holiday. It's the only three-week vacation we've had as a family. It was full of adventure for sure with the car accident, the boat accident (I'll go into it later.) and when we returned from Glasgow and picking up the girls, we discovered someone had broken into our cottage and stolen money, the girl's camera, and they broke the 50 pence machine that we needed to have heat. Of course, all the stuff we'd packed in the boat coming over had to be put on top of the car on our return trip. Plus, due to the car accident, the only way I could get in and out of the front passenger seat was to crawl out the driver's side. What a disaster. You may be surprised to hear that I still find Scotland charming and my favorite place in Europe. The people are so friendly, and the scenery is breathtaking.

August 18, 1986 - I started a 15-week course with Duke last Tuesday. After only one lesson, he walks on the line so much better because *I* learned so much. The classes are free from the local dog club. There are 8 in the class. We had a grill with 16 adults & 4 children, people we'd met through work, fun.

August 19, 1986 - For our grill party, I rented tables & chairs & we sat out from 7 p.m. - 3 a.m. They were all businesspeople from Bensheim except Jenny & Peter Schmeide. I have so much fruit in the garden - apples, pears, black raspberries & yellow plums (Mirabellen in German).

August 27, 1986 - Duke ate holes in the pine kitchen hutch Ian made years ago. He also chewed all three cushions to our big grey sofa with white balls of stuffing covering the living room floor. Dang, we can't afford a new sofa nor to recover it at the moment! Claire is learning knitting in school.

September 13, 1986 - I had my first car accident, a 19-year-old ran into the back of my car. His car was totaled. No paint or body damage to my car but will cost about DM 250. He will pay so it doesn't have to go through his insurance. I went to Ian's office to do a bit of work today and opened the mail to find a check for DM 103,000! Thank God! Both accounts are finally in the black! Ian's got so much to do before Japan it's ridiculous. He was in Munich for two days this week. Monday he'll be in Austria for 3 days. Then Berlin for 2 days (wish I could go along) & Holland for one day. He leaves for Japan Friday October 3rd & returns October 15th. October 16th it will be 13 years since I met him in Moscow. And I still think he's a knockout. Not bad, eh?"

October 3, 1986 - The dollar is incredibly low now at DM2 = $1.

October 6, 1986 - David Taylor started working at Anaspec last week. It's sure nice to be able to speak English at work. I've decided to give the English Discussion Group a rest after all these years. I've been going since 1978. I started a German course which meets once a week mainly to learn how words are spelled, so it is more for writing German, but of course spoken German is also part of the course.

October 18, 1986 - I made over 50 liters of apple juice today. I took them to a man in the Odenwald who has a hydraulic press and got the juice straight away. He only charged DM10. A neighbor loaned me a 60-litre plastic container and I then brought it home and heated the juice up, 30 liters at a time, to 80 degrees and put them in wine bottles. It tastes great. Ian's trip to Japan was evidently successful. It's extremely expensive there. He said it costs DM10 to fart! I know it's been over three years since we've been to the states, but there also never seems to be enough money for four plane tickets either. Ian earns quite a good salary, but we never have any money. Heather phoned and she's coming Nov 5-12.

October 27, 1986 - I can now buy English cheddar in Bensheim. A very interesting development with German TV. It is now possible to get the original language on films by pushing the right button on our remote control we can get films in English or French or whatever. It's great! Cable TV is also coming to Bensheim, but I don't know how much it will cost.

November 4, 1986 - There is a slump in the market now. Nobody seems to be getting orders. Hope it doesn't last too long. Money for research must be tight.

November 14, 1986 - was checking out prices for Andrea & Claire to fly to the states next summer. I have promised them that when they are both 10 years old, they could fly together without me. Prices will be about DM 1,200 each round trip.

January 5, 1987 - Ian gave me a radio for the kitchen, long, medium & short wave so I get BBC news. Duke pulled down the Christmas tree, ate the lights, several decorations & chewed two holes in the very valued Christmas tree skirt that Georgie made me. I have proudly shown it off every year for over 10 years. Yet, and get this, Duke graduated at the *top* of his class on December 9th in obedience school. I'm going to continue with an advanced course so that he'll walk alongside me and not run away and all in all learn to be a well-behaved dog. Not sure how to train him not to eat wood and fabric furniture.

January 13, 1987 - It's been -20 C that's -4F for the past few days and it's reached -40, that's the same in F & C in other parts of Europe. Bloody cold, by standards here. You wouldn't believe it, but Dad called on Saturday. I haven't talked to him for 2½ years! Ian fired secretary #4 last week for incompetence.

January 15, 1987 - You can understand why Claire wrote in her thank you letter that she would wait to change the money you sent because the exchange rate is going up. The $10 you sent for her 8th birthday, she got DM35. Two years later, she will only get DM18.

January 23, 1987 - Ian's working on a very complicated air bearing system, which he hopes will be successful in a big way.

February 11, 1987 - I'm having medical tests for my thyroid issues. I don't know if I've told you but there have been very few orders coming in since late October. And it's made a big hiccough in our cash flow. But the biggest problem is that Candella, the company in England that ordered three massive systems last year, has gone bankrupt. We delivered two systems & have completed the 3rd. But they have only paid for the 1st system. It's over DM 80,000 so it really *hurts*! We don't know when or if we'll ever get the money. I just phoned about tickets for Andrea and Claire. They will cost a bit less than I previously mentioned, about DM 900 each.

February 26, 1987 - Results of my thyroid test, I must have an operation to remove 2 cysts which the doctor said could "explode" at any time. Duke was poisoned by eating something in the field, spent 2 days at vet.

March 10, 1987 - "As the "foreign" contact for the Hemsberg Schule I've welcomed two parents of new children in Claire's class. It's exactly 10 years this month that we arrived in Germany. Doesn't seem possible.

March 18, 1987 - April 1 is the 7th anniversary of Anaspec. Our cleaning lady quit, and the new secretary hasn't started yet so I'm doing both. There's a reason some people call me a "Tausandfußler" that, literally translated, means someone with 1000 feet, but the real meaning is like the "Jack of all Trades" saying. Business is picking up, thank heavens. It's snowed about 10 inches yesterday, but it's nearly melted now. That's very unusual.

April 12, 1987 - I booked the flight for Andrea, Claire & Rainer, a neighbor boy who spent time at Sharon's farm. They fly June 19th and return July 16th. Andrea must pay full price - DM 1,199 and Claire DM 900. I think the $/DM rate is the lowest in seven years, $1.75 = DM1. Ian likes his Saab 9000 Turbo. June called. She'll be here in 3 days.

April 18, 1987 - Cousin Candy and I have had fun, especially on our tour of southern Germany where we saw the famous fairytale castle, Neuschwanstein. I took her to the airport today.

July 1, 1987 - Hope the girls are doing well. How is their money holding out?

July 8, 1987 - to the folks & A & C - We are going to Austria Fri. - Sun. to scout out places for our Christmas skiing holiday. On Thursday, July 23rd, Daddy (Ian) & I are driving to England for a few days of sailing. We had a very nice meal last night at the Burggraf in Auerbach. Yesterday, I made strawberry jam. I will make red currant jam today. Duke was very naughty Monday night. He chewed the Gelände (banister) and the second step downstairs. Andrea, if you get a chance, buy an organ book of American songs.

August 3, 1987 - Claire started at her new school, the AKG Gymnasium; there are 25 in her class, 5 girls & 20 boys. She has 33 hours a week, 7:55 a.m.-1:05 p.m. M-F + 4 hours Saturday. Andrea has classes until 1 each day except Thur. Ann & Bill are coming for two weeks next week. A & C left their tennis shoes in MN. Is it worth it $$-wise to send them?

August 17, 1987 - Ian has booked us a two-week Christmas skiing holiday in Austria. I hope no one breaks a leg! I haven't had problems with my legs since the varicose vein operation.

October 26, 1987 - Claire is having her adenoids out November 3rd. She's had bronchitis for a month and has missed a lot of school. Andrea is receiving tutoring in German and math. It's DM 11/hr. Ian & I are flying to London November 7th-12th. Bill has moved premises and there's a "grand opening."

November 10, 1987 - I'm so blessed to go along with Ian for his business trip to Israel. Everything is incredibly interesting. We go to Jerusalem Wednesday. Shalom. Ian is working all week. He'll only have one free day. But I can walk around anywhere. It's fascinating.

November 11, 1987 - We're sitting on the beach with beer & pita bread looking out at the Mediterranean Sea.

Christmas Letter 1987 - I've started teaching conversational English to two German doctors, Frau & Herr Doktors Barbara & Roland Jost. Claire is in gymnasium. Andrea's taking organ lessons and gymnastics. We had an interesting trip to Israel. My imagination of "Oh, Little Town of Bethlehem" will never be the same. It was filthy and I got my bottom slapped (hard!) by about a 13-year-old Arab boy as we passed walking down the steps past a market.

January 1, 1988 - postcard Saalbach - super fireworks last night for 40 min. Had 10 days of lessons, lots of bruises, aches & pains, and a great time skiing! I wish I'd started years ago!

January 20, 1988 - I got a rabbit hutch for free and we got Claire a rabbit. She told me a while ago that since her 6th birthday, every time she blew out the candles on her cake she wished for a rabbit. That kind of tugged at the old heart. Keks, the bunny, (German for biscuit) and Duke have not yet met. Good thing I have been going to ski gymnastics once a week since September. One of the most interesting parts about our skiing holiday was meeting people from all over the world: Australia, South Africa, Denmark, Sweden, Norway, Finland, England, the States, etc.

February 9, 1988 - I'm coming about July 25 for three weeks! The girls are going for two weeks on a horse-riding holiday and Ian will watch them for the 3rd week.

February 23, 1988 - I haven't booked my trip to U.S. yet but will make it for August Ian said he'd like to take them away for a week on his own–maybe to Switzerland. I will be in MN next summer for my 25th class reunion and the double wedding of Doug & Leigh & Bonnie & Dave Mahar–at Faith Haven. Three weeks in MN & one week in CA

March 11, 1988 - Donna & David Grover are supposed to arrive in a week.

March 20, 1988 - Herzliche Ostergrüße - Easter card - Am teaching English to five different people (DM 25/hr per person) once a week. So, I'll be able to earn my own pocket money for the states!

March 30, 1988 - Since December, I'm making DM 500/month tax-free. After Easter, I'm starting an English Club at Andrea's school. Ian got rid of the mumbling engineer who no one understood and got a real nice young man to replace him. That makes eight full-time employees and me.

April 18, 1988 - We haven't heard from Dad for months. I've written two letters with no answer. Ian has finally gotten a FAX machine. I was wondering if you know anyone in Battle Lake or Ashby who also has one? Maybe the bank? It is so cheap and quick. I could send you a letter and it would be there immediately. It works on the telephone lines and copies this page size in a matter of seconds.

May 26, 1988 - Had the second migraine of my life. The first was when I was married to Steve Anderson. Awful.

June 8, 1988 - I bought a Trachten (German traditional costume) outfit for my 25th class reunion next month.

July 12, 1988 - Nan has only one working kidney, both she & Jeanne James are very ill.

August 19, 1988 - Aunt Al gave me her silverplate set for 12 in a nice wooden box. It will be heavy, but I'm taking it back with me.

August 19, 1988 - We had Thanksgiving with turkey and dressing and mashed potatoes and cranberries. Roy, Tiny, Wendy, and Ray were here plus Aunt Al, Grandma Jo, Candy & me. It was just great.

August 28, 1988 - Thanks for the super holiday; Ian, A & C returned from Austria.

August 30, 1988 - At the office since 9:30 a.m. and it's gone 3 p.m. already. Ian has an important customer today and they just got back from lunch. If he pulls it off, it will be his biggest order yet - over DM 300,000!

September 26, 1988 - Went to Switzerland at the weekend for a mini getaway. We've decided that it is *the* place to retire! The girls and I are going to England for the fall break October 21-29.

October 3, 1988 - Weekend before last we took off and went to Weggis, Küstnacht and Lucerne, Switzerland for two days. It's a four-hour drive. We're going skiing again at Christmas. Ian is tired. He's working so hard, weekends & late still–for 8 years now! The girls have school on Saturdays. I've got another single pupil (teaching conversational English)–a Vietnamese man who's going to the states in three weeks. Plus, a group of four to five women.

October 14, 1988 – Bensheim–Anaspec letter marking Loyd's birthday sent via fax from Anaspec office. "I was chosen by the parents of Andrea's class to be the 'parent's representative' at the equivalent of the PTA. My first 'job' was to talk to a teacher who has been yelling and belittling the girls. He is an Army officer instructor in the afternoons, so he obviously has a problem switching from soldiers to students! I was very nervous before the meeting, but I did quite well. He promised me he would try to be better!!! How about that?! He admitted that he sometimes uses names and expressions that are perhaps not acceptable. That is an understatement.

December 15, 1988 - a lovely Christmas card with a watercolor of Bensheim Marktplatz by artist Herbert Haydin. Claire has impossible behavior lately. She's so hardheaded. Now where did she get *that* from?!

January 2, 1989 - Saalbach, Austria We're skiing up a storm and have advanced from the easy (blue) slopes to medium (red) which is obviously more challenging.

January 23, 1989 - Claire had a nice birthday party–10 girls, bowling & out for pizzas. It was the 25th children's bd party I've organized, so I decided to splurge.

Valentine's Day 1989 - Claire is going to start taking saxophone lessons. We're lucky that she can borrow one for free from the school to see if she likes it. Then we'll have to buy one for around DM 1,500-2,000! Andrea & I have been taking organ lessons for three years now. Claire quit after the first year.

March 8, 1989 - Eureka! Our bathroom–totally remodeled–is finished! The bidet must be replaced because it was chipped, but I had my first bath last night with a glass of champagne!

April 10, 1989 - making bread - white & whole wheat

May 22, 1989 - Ian is almost ready to deliver a big order to the Hamburg Observatory. I had to go to Frankfurt airport to pick up Prof. Dr. de Vent, the head of the agency.

June 7, 1989 - We're here on the stand of the Laser Opto-Elektronik Internationale Seminare und Ausstellung in München (Munich). It's not as busy as it was two years ago. But maybe today it will pick up. Most interest is on our new product - air bearing systems.

June 20, 1989 - We're at the hospital waiting for the doctor to look at Claire's ring finger. Doctor had to "set" her finger, she's not too pleased. Ian has worked every day since February without a break, weekends & holidays, too. We're getting a visit from Kaye Braaten's two daughters (22 & 23).

July 16, 1989 - Glad to hear June & Randy are finally separating. Have you booked your flight for October yet? I'm dying for some Aunt Jemima pancake mix. I've got syrup. Garrison Keillor's book, *Leaving Home*, is terrific.

Part IV: August 1989 - July 1994

It takes courage to grow up and
become who you really are.

e. e. cummings

NOTE: Despite starting off with a great sailing trip to the Greek Isles, our lives were destined to change drastically when the Berlin Wall came down on November 9th, 1989. Money that our customers formerly invested in our products was destined for the former East Germany. Things altered so fast with no planning by the German government for all the social and economic changes that would result from the reunification of East and West Germany. Ian considered and then finally sold our company after continuing to experience dire financial straits for fifteen years. Thankfully, I had a lot of pleasure in tending our large garden with huge fruit trees. But my biggest accomplishment was a result of me walking into our local newspaper office, the Bergstraße Echo, to complain about a new change in their layout. It was an act that would lead to my favorite job: being a full-time freelance photojournalist for six dailies and one weekly German newspaper, owned by the same company. Unfortunately, it wasn't enough to hold our family together. On the contrary, in retrospect, it probably added to the end of our 20-year marriage.

September 10th, 1989 - We'll be sailing the Greek Isles a week from today. On Saturday, we're flying to Corfu for a weeks' sailing on a 40-ft yacht with Bill Vince (Ian's partner) & Jenny (his girlfriend).

September 21, 1989 - This is without question the most fabulous one-week holiday Ian & I have ever had. The Ionian Islands of Greece are stark, primitive, beautiful & parts look nearly untouched for the past few hundred years. I've taken over 100 photos and will do a show & tell when you come. We fly back tomorrow. I'm a bit sunburned. Temp. is @ 90 degrees F. We just sailed past Skorpio (Onassis' Island!) Didn't see anybody rich nor famous!"

September 25th, 1989 - Looking forward to your & Loyd visiting in three weeks

December 2, 1989 - Andrea really likes her bike, which cost DM 400, she paid DM 100 towards it. She has started guitar lessons and loves it. She has stopped organ lessons. So, we'll be getting her a guitar for Christmas. Claire's getting a tennis racket. Also, they'll each be receiving luggage sets. We leave Friday, the 22nd for our skiing vacation to Austria. We stay overnight near Munich to break up the trip. We come back January 6th.

December 11, 1989 - Ian had to be in Wiesbaden at 8 a.m. for his boat test which lasts until 4:30 p.m. Heather arrives on Thursday. It's wonderful for mankind about the Berlin Wall coming down on November 9, 1989.

January 8, 1990 - We returned from our skiing holiday in Austria early due to lack of snow, unfortunately.

January 9, 1990 - I still haven't been to Berlin in all the 13 years we've lived here. The financial drain on West Germany is enormous now. It's fabulous that the East is loosening its tethers, but it's costing us. There is resentment here and there. But basically, people are breathing easier.

February 18, 1990 – Nan (she's our former neighbor, Jeanne James' daughter) died in January, kidney cancer. David & Donna Grover came on their blitz tour of Europe and spent one day with us. Claire is going to Belgium as part of a school choir competition. The number they must sing is in Dutch! Andrea is excited that her friend, Nadine Ringenwald, will be able to go with her to Italy–Lake Maggoire–for her ten-day holiday in July. A group from the Bensheim sports club is going so it's relatively cheap at DM 350. Ian is going to Yugoslavia for one week in June with David to take his final sailing test. Claire is going with Ira to Finland for three weeks in July-August. I've decided to have my hair cut short and with a perm on top.

March 19, 1990 - Andrea has a French exchange friend, Gullianne. My friend, Carola Munkes, has a daughter Ira, who is Claire's friend. We FINALLY got a huge check today, so Ian could pay his December & January salaries (note this March!) Luckily the orders have really been coming in fast this year so the cash flow will be better. On Saturday, Ian is celebrating ten years with Anaspec. We're having a special dinner and wine tasting for fourteen people at the Fürstenlager in Auerbach, the royal Hessen family's summer residence. I have a new outfit. It's fabulous, from Paris, the new marine look, white jacket, and blouse with a long Navy skirt with anchors and chains. Claire's and Ian's trip to England was a very special time. When he was telling me about it, he got tears in his eyes, so I know it meant a lot to him. They've been playing squash every Sunday since January, too. It's nice that he's finally getting to know his kids. Andrea is not interested in playing squash. For a present, I'm giving Ian a large frame with currencies from 18 different countries with which he's done business in the past 10 years. Germany, U.S., Israel, Japan, France, Belgium, Holland,

Austria, Switzerland, Soviet Union, Korea, Finland, Italy, Portugal, Canada, Scotland, and Northern Ireland. So, he'll never again have to say there's no money–ha ha!

April 7, 1990 - Dorothy & Bob Eckert from Wahpeton have spent the day with us. Bob was states attorney when I worked at the Daily News. He has been a judge for the past 15 years. I've had a rotten week. David handed in his notice on Monday. He'll be leaving us at the end of June. Of course, it means lots more work for Ian. He won't be replacing David. He's decided to get a salesman.

April 14, 1990 - The BIG NEWS is that they finally hooked up our cable TV which means we now have @ 25 channels instead of four. We have two with English news & programs, two sports, two music, three French, two in German to watch breakfast news, European business news at 6 a.m. which is usually when we wake up and have our tea in bed.

April 19, 1990 - The garden is looking beautiful. That's my therapy at the moment. I really enjoy working in it and the rewards are now paying off. It sure is nice to have more choices to watch TV.

June 4, 1990 - We are having another cash flow hiccough. Honestly, I'm sick of this money situation, or rather the lack thereof. Ian works so damn hard and yet there never seems to be any money. His overhead is tremendous & he says we are not getting things out the door fast enough, nor sold high enough. What a vicious circle.

June 23, 1990 - I started singing in a group in Schwanheim, a small village next to Bensheim. The choir is mixed and all ages, songs are religious as well as traditional, mostly German, with some English and Latin. Checkpoint Charlie was dismantled last Friday, that's really something. David's last day is this Friday. We're in another cash flow pit which is depressing as hell. No paycheck since March.

June 26, 1990 - Ian and I are going to Vienna for 5 days on Saturday for business!!!

July 2, 1990 -We're going to *Phantom of the Opera* tonight. Ian's taking the day off tomorrow and we're going for a riverboat ride on the Danube.

July 10, 1990 - Claire is off to Finland today until August 6th. Andrea's going to Lake Garda on the Swiss/Italian border for two weeks. Ian has decided to go to England on his own. I can't help feeling rather hurt that he doesn't seem to need/want me along. On my birthday, Ian didn't even give me a card, let alone a present.

July 20, 1990 - We had a dreadful accident at the factory on Monday. Our foreman, Herr Germs, had the first joints of two fingers on his left hand cut off by a large piece of granite that slipped from its belt on the crane. He'll be off at least four weeks. With another sick, David gone and two on holiday, it's a real problem.

August 15, 1990 - We're getting back to normal after Candy's visit and the girl's holidays. Candy and I went to Neuschwanstein - the fairytale castle in southern Germany. It was fantastic, but high season and full of tourists. We spent 3.5 hours going to 26 different places to find a room. We finally went over the border to Austria and found a room straight away. We took the back roads home driving eight hours instead of about four. Ian and I are driving to Yugoslavia to go sailing for the first week in September. The couple we'd hoped to go with can't go so we've invited Ian's cousin's son, William, to come with us. Ian sure needs the break. But I must say, since David left, he's coming home at very reasonable times between

5 - 6 p.m. It used to be 7:30 - 9 p.m. The girls start school on August 20th. Finances have picked up a bit, but they are still not brilliant. Ian needs a break. We're going to where Ian took his license in June. Andrea is staying with our neighbor, Frau Schmank. Claire is staying with a class friend. I've decided I'm having Duke fixed when we get back. Maybe he'll stop barking so much.

October 10, 1990 - We have set up a darkroom in the upstairs' back bathroom. Heather is coming in a week. I think she plans to cheer me up. It'll be nice to have her here so I can think about something other than money–or rather the lack of it!!! The dollar/DM rate is awful; I think it's $1 = DM 1.53. The price of gas is outrageous. We are paying nearly DM 1.47/liter.

October 11, 1990 - Thought I'd write and tell you how things are. Bloody awful is one description. Desperate is another. We are a hair's breadth away from bankruptcy and my gut is in knots. Everything we own is tied up in the company. We have just re-mortgaged our house and are waiting for the DM 50,000 to "lend" the company which is stretched to the limit in credit at all three of our banks. One of Ian's customers owes him nearly DM 50,000, but says he is still "testing the system" and won't pay–even though Ian has installed it and it is working. Ian has not paid his salary for six months and his and my personal accounts are over DM 30,000 overdrawn. We still are remaining sane, but I don't know for how long Ian, nor I can stand this pressure. This morning for the first time, he said the pressure would kill him if it continued. Ian has lots of orders and so many people are interested in his new measuring system, it's almost laughable, but we need more orders now and pre-partial payments. If ever anybody needed a miracle, boy, it is us. I'm trying for everyone's sake to keep my cool, but I need some type of help, too. Believe me, I've also been praying. I sure could use a tape from you with some positive thoughts, perhaps some good news and a laugh or two. Please take the time, I need you.

October 30, 1990 - Frau Schmank will be 90 on Monday. We had a tree episode with our nasty neighbors who live between Frau Schmank and us.

November 29, 1990 - Ian's being sued. He got two nice orders yesterday. And he's going to Montreal in January where there is a possible half a million-mark order. Cross your fingers!

December 7, 1990 - Ian's in Hannover. He has received the first of what he hopes are many orders from Canada. 1990 has been a great year for Germany, but it's sure one year I'd like to forget on a personal level. Andrea was 15 this week. Amazing. We got her clothes. She says she wants to change her image going off the sloppy look. Now that you have your house on Eagle Lake on the market, what are you going to ask for the house and how much property goes with it?

January 21, 1991 - Today is Grandma's 90th birthday. - Claire invited eight friends to her birthday party, but it started snowing about 3 p.m. and by 6, when everyone should have been here, it was quite bad, two kids didn't make it. I even had to go pick up two boys as their parents didn't dare drive in the snow. It was only a few centimeters for heaven's sake! But the kids who came had a good time and they went out about 10:30 and had a snowball fight in the garden.

January 28, 1991 - Just when I was trying desperately to THINK POSITIVE, we've been dealt another blow, not one but two. Two weeks ago, Herr Schmidt, our technician and fine mechanic of three years resigned. He got a job closer to his home. Then last week,

Willy, our hole driller & all-around best worker for four and a half years turned in his notice. It's enough to scare me, I can tell you. That plus our massive overdrawn bank accounts. I just don't know how Ian carries on & I pray to God he doesn't one day just flip out. He must beg for every pfennig owed him which is currently over DM 200,000! Everyone else seems to be down to the line financially, too. Now it will be more difficult than ever to get products out of the door fast as we'll be training two people for months. Andrea & Claire took a three-day (3-6 p.m.) self-defense course over the weekend. GOOD NEWS FINALLY–Two good things happened this morning. We got checks in for DM 60,000. Thank God & Ian hired a replacement fine mechanic. He can start next week which is very good because Herr Schmidt will have several weeks with him to train before leaving.

February 21, 1991 - Ian has booked a sailing holiday to Yugoslavia from June 29 - July 13. We certainly can't afford this, so I don't know why he does it other than that he'd go crazy if he didn't have something positive to look forward to. I mean if & when he's able to pay back his back salary–all 9 months of it–I told him I desperately want to go to the states for the Battle Lake Centennial. He says I should go. We can't afford that either. However, I, too, think I'd go crazy if I didn't have something pleasant to look forward to. So, I've booked a flight to Mpls. from July 19th to August 5th. I'm paying for the ticket from the English lessons I am giving, a few dollars each month. I haven't even told Ian I've booked it yet. It's very important to him that all four of us go on this sailing holiday because he believes by next summer, Andrea & Claire will want to go their own ways for holidays as they get older.

April 14, 1991 – Thinking about your upcoming birthday on the 24th. I want you to know you have been the best mother possible and, in fact, I would have chosen you to be my mother. When I see other people and how they relate to their parents and children, siblings, and relatives, I feel so blessed to have the family I've had. That goes all the way around from you to Dad to Loyd, my sisters, my kids and even my ex-husbands. I love all the people in my life, and they have all contributed greatly to me. And no one gave me as much as you. You gave me courage, integrity, strength, power, self-confidence, humor, a never give up attitude and the foundations of my faith. For all that and much, much more, I thank God that you are my mother.

May 3, 1991 - Claire has her first big jazz band concert on May 28th, at the Park Theatre in Bensheim. Ian is going, too. Ingrid Wood won an extra ticket to the Fats Domino concert in Bensheim and gave it to me as she & Mike already had tickets. Fats was just great. We'll be going to the Munich exhibit June 9 - 16th. The girls will stay on their own.

June 10, 1991 - We're at LASER '91 in Munich for a week.

July 1991 - *I miss Minnesota!* That's the name of the series of four blogs about MN I started writing. The first ones are about learning a foreign language, the three-tier school system in Germany, no extracurricular activities in schools, and driving on the autobahn.

August 8, 1991 - I taught the girls how to play Spite & Malice tonight.

August 28, 1991 - I have set up an office in the top bathroom annex which is also my darkroom. Ian generously allowed me to take a computer from the office. Yee gads, prices are going up. Petrol is DM1.49/liter. Interest rates have gone up to 14%. It costs me DM 75 to fill my tank. Claire had a bike accident. She has taken on the cleaning lady's job at the factory and is paid DM10/hr. She works about four hours a week, so she can now start buying some of her own clothes. Claire at 14 cleans every bit as good as our past cleaning ladies if not better. Both girls are taking Italian at the local evening school. Andrea is also taking typing which is not offered in school.

September 30, 1991 - Andrea was in a car accident and ended up in hospital in Heppenheim. Then Ian stepped on steel swarth which went through his shoe & through his foot. He had to be rushed to the ER.

October 6, 1991 - Andrea is better. Claire is invited to a party by an 18-year-old who has a car and is of legal drinking age! I said she could go, but that I'd pick her up as everyone else was staying the night.

October 28, 1991 - Our trip to England was fun, mostly. Dad commented to Ann, his sister-in-law, that his children treat him like he is dead. After hearing that, I decided to make one more effort to see them. So, when I arrived at Heather's on Sunday afternoon, I rang them to ask if the girls and I could come and see them on Tuesday. Maureen answered the phone and I talked only to her. I asked her to please ask Dad if we could come. I said I wouldn't come if we weren't wanted. She said, you're wanted–without hesitation. But I asked her to please check with Dad. She asked him and he said yes. The next morning, I got a fretful call from Ann (who obviously felt very uncomfortable being in the middle saying Dad had rung to say he did NOT want us to come. He'd had a sleepless night and was very upset. He told her he's had six happy years with Maureen and doesn't want that to change. I didn't know what he thought was going to happen. In any case, we did not go and that, as far as I am concerned, is really the end. Andrea was very hurt. She had been looking forward to seeing him. Claire was relieved. She did not want to go at all. After spending the afternoon with Penny, Andrea has gone vegetarian. Have I written about Claire's boyfriend, Lars? He's 18 and in his last year at the AKG. They met at dancing lessons. Andrea doesn't have a boyfriend, but she goes out with friends on Fridays and Saturdays. So now I don't close an eye until they get in at 11:30. And in six weeks, it'll be 12 midnight for Andrea when she turns 16. The latest with Ian the weekend we got back from England: Ian told me he has decided to sell the whole thing–land and building. He is very down. He works so very hard, and his overdraft has just gotten so big, he can't get it down. The irony of it is that the company is making money this year just not enough. He has got his costs way, way down over last year and he is making a profit. But there is the constant pressure of not knowing if the banks are going to pull the rug out at any minute–plus not knowing if he can meet his payroll each month. He went to his bank manager who said he'd first have to talk to his tax adviser. So, he saw his tax man and he told Ian he would have to pay a profit tax of–you guessed it! DM 500,000! So, he was back to square one again. The result is that he must put the field next to the factory up for sale offering about 3,000 sq. meters to the highest bidder at about DM180 a sq. meter. He bought it 5 years ago for DM18/ a sq. meter. At the end of last week, he had an order for DM 100,000 from Holland. He could do with about three more like that.

November 13, 1991 - I'm devastated to hear that Loyd died in his sleep November 11th.

November 20, 1991 - Here's my list of items I'd love you to bring next month: Dentyne gum, marshmallows, Johnson's Baby Powder with cornstarch, Cheerios, saltine crackers, crunchy peanut butter - well, you *did* ask!

January 7, 1992 -I asked Sharon to look up contact information for several press publications like *National Association of Freelance Writers and Photographers* and *Magazine Writers.* Got my first two rejection letters from *Minnesota Monthly* and *Mpls. -St. Paul Magazine.* Included one of my new business cards Barbara La Valleur-Purvis, MCIJ Freelance Writer, Photographer, Editor. The initials MCIJ is the Chartered Institute of Journalists in London that I joined. I also got a press card from them.

January 12, 1992 - I've written an article about Andrea's car accident for *Guidepost* and sent it off.

January 28, 1992 - Ian made a Harley Davidson CD holder for Claire, it took him three days! I received a couple more rejection letters including one from *Modern Maturity.*

February 18, 1992 - Today I got my Press Card issued by the British Royal Chartered Institute of Journalists. It cost me £80 a year, but I think it will be worth it. We'll see. Ian sold his land (2,800 sq. meters) and got DM165/sq. meter. What a pity all the money must go to pay off the overdrawn account. Still, he will be relieved when it all goes through. Claire is doing the sailing course because, in Greece, two people need a license for sailing a boat.

March 9, 1992 - Andrea has been accepted to do her Abitur. That's the academic level comparable to the International Baccalaureate, the GCE Advanced Level, and the Advanced Placement tests. In England, it's called A levels.

March 26, 1992 - I gave my resume to the City of Bensheim public relations woman. A couple of weeks later, she phoned and asked me if I wanted to do some color photos for a brochure.

March 29, 1992 - Claire starts her practical sailing course today. For the next seven weeks, she will have to go for two hours, four times a week to a small lake in Heppenheim where the boat club has dinghies. Luckily, she is picked up and brought home by an older man who is taking the course and drives right by our house and who is her "partner" in the practical sailing part.

April 14, 1992 - Ingrid is filling in as part-time secretary for Ian. Claire passed her sailing license test. It only took her 20 minutes. When Ian did his two years ago, he needed more than the allotted 60 min. I have spent quite a lot setting myself up with equipment to freelance: a new Nikon camera body DM 800, filters, film, business cards, stickers, paper, stamps, not to mention the hours and hours I've invested and so far, I've only made DM 500. The most depressing word in the English language to me is MONEY.

April 28, 1992 - A lot of garden work with two huge yellow cherry trees, apple and pear trees, tulips, roses, lilac bush, daffodils. My weed pulling arm is so sore, wondering if it's arthritis? Gez, I'm not even fifty yet. Life is unfair! Claire is still plugging away at her practical sailing experience. I don't think she's had a free day over the Easter holidays. On Sunday, Ian and I went over and watched her for about an hour. I would have been scared sh--less as the dinghy looked like it would tip several times!! I'm taking photos of the May 1st national holiday Wanderung (10 k. walk) on the Bergstraße through the vineyards. They're for a brochure, the guy will pay me DM 600-800 for three to four photos. Yeah!

May 18, 1992 - Claire and her sailing partner were sent out as the first ones to take their test. They left at 7:15 a.m. and didn't get back until nearly 6 p.m. Andrea is in Italy with her class for a week. I have discovered that one of the local editors of the paper we read lives two houses away. He's lived there for nearly four years, and I just found out about it two weeks ago and now he is moving to a new apartment in a couple of months. Anyway, he is very nice and interested in my story on Frau Schmank, which I have even re-done in bloody German, if you can believe that! I'm also re-doing the German boating license story that I was supposed to do "on spec" for the editor of Yachting. She returned it last week saying, "Sorry, but the German license piece isn't quite suitable." She didn't tell me why.

May 29, 1992 - I'm on a tour to Czechoslovakia with the Schwanheim choir. We saw buildings today in Prague that were constructed before the discovery of America. Wow. There is a great deal of renovating going on & there are pickpockets *everywhere*– even at the cathedral shown here & in the centuries' old Jewish cemetery.

May 30, 1992 - I STARTED WORK AS A FREELANCE PHOTOJOURNALIST! I have my article about Frau Schmank being a substitute for A & C whose Grandmother lives in California. My first photo and story + a photo of me appeared in the Bergstraße Echo.

May 31, 1992 - Bernd Sterzelmaier, our neighbor, who would eventually become my boss, rang our doorbell & said, "Grab your camera and come quick." He wanted me to take a photo of the Euler paper factory. They were dismantling a 55-meter-high brick chimney which was being replaced by a steel one. It was quite a photo and, of course, was in the paper the next day.

June 23, 1992 - Enjoying our sailing trip with Ian, Claire & Nicole from Corfu to Paxos and Antipaxos, Greece.

July 2, 1992 - We arrived at the border of Yugoslavia on June 19th - the day war broke out. They wouldn't let us in the country. Our boat was towed to Grado, Italy, so we could get on the boat & we're now sailing in Italian waters. The best part of the trip was sailing into Venice. Wow! The downside is that the Italian coast is flat and boring compared to the Yugoslavia coast which is rugged and interesting with old buildings you can see from the boat. The worst part was that the water in and around Venice and the northern coast is full of *raw sewage*, just gross to look at. Obviously, we couldn't go swimming in it like we could on the northern coast of Yugoslavia.

July 15, 1992 - I had a few friends over for my birthday last week. We had coffee, cake, and champagne. One of my friends told a story that was just too good to be true so the next day I made a few calls to check out some facts and got a story out of it. She and her 14-year-old daughter were walking in the woods behind their house in a village outside of Heppenheim when they saw a kangaroo. Yes, a real kangaroo! They couldn't believe their eyes. They learned that it had escaped from a local zoo. Unfortunately, the editing changed my article in such a way that the humor was lost. Oh, well. At least I got a byline which is not given that often. Ian even got a faxed copy of it which had appeared in a newspaper in the Odenwald read by Ute who used to work with Ian. Yesterday, I interviewed a man in Bensheim who for the past two years has been building a massive sailboat in his backyard. Every time I go to one of our supermarkets, EKZ, I drive by it. So, one day I stopped and talked to the owner. I'm amazed that no one has done an article about it before. The first time I taped the interview on Ian's small hand recorder, so having just awakened Andrea, I've given her the job of transcribing the 1.5

hr. interview on the Dictaphone. She's thrilled. It's good practice for her typing, besides, both A & C are showing signs of boredom already and the school holidays still have three weeks to go! I sympathize with you selling your place and moving. Whenever we have had to move, I became hardened and unsentimental and threw things away. As it's been over six years since that has happened–the longest ever for me–I'm overdue for a big turnout. Nothing new with merger. Everything takes ages. Will keep you posted. Ian was very depressed after coming back from sailing. He would just as soon have stayed there. He's currently a bear to live with.

August 2, 1992 - I'm up in the darkroom developing film. Andrea just had a visit from Hassan. Yesterday was the annual Bensheim Flea Market. I was there at 5:30 a.m. setting up. I made DM 240. Unfortunately, I stepped on the edge of the curb and my knee popped out, luckily it popped back in as I fell down screaming. It's swollen and hurts. I will probably have to have it x-rayed. Still nothing new with the company. I try not to think about it. Sending a Greek story and photos off to Yachting Magazine in New York.

September 2, 1992 - Barb Wasson Dahms is coming the 12th and going back the 25th. I'm totally busy and doing things every minute. I got my first translation job this week for the city of Bensheim. It will be a kit for tour operators about things to do and see in Bensheim. It is 19 pages. When that's done, I'll translate a brochure on Bensheim used for a walking tour explaining points of interest. I get DM 50 an hour for that. I asked for–and got–a raise yesterday as it was September 1 and I had been at the paper for 3 months. Really happy working for the Bergstraße Echo, Darmstädter Echo & Südhessiche Post. The two things that are turning up short are housework and garden work. Claire helps with ironing. Andrea pitches in as does Ian.

September 14, 1992 -Barb Wasson Dahms & I were in King's College, Cambridge this morning, we are now in Lincoln on the way to York. I'm driving Ian's car.

September 19, 1992 - Barb & I had the best time imaginable in England and Scotland, just under 4,000 km. The day after she arrived, we left for Felixstowe at 4:30 a.m. Thankfully, I was able to pay for my trip with the money I've saved for the past three years from my English lessons. I took over 800 photos on our trip, mostly color slides, but also about 150 b & w.

December 17, 1992 - We're meeting Heather & John & family on Christmas Eve at the Hotel de France in Montreuil-sur- Mer, located near the coast south of Bologna. It's the first time we've done a holiday together.

February 4, 1993 - I'm in my office/darkroom/bathroom and I'm hardly home these days. I'm working a lot at the newspapers. Andrea and Claire are independent and make their own meals, thankfully. I've officially hired Claire as my cleaning lady as she 1. does the job well 2. needs the money and 3. is trustworthy. She was happy to quit her part-time job as her boss is a real a. h. She works about five hours a week and I pay her DM 10 which is about $2.60/hr. Both girls had lousy report cards this time. Hopefully, it is a phase. There is a definite lack of motivation there. Their rooms are a TIP.

February 9, 1993 - The amount of time I'm spending on my photo show is incredible. I have bought the latest enlarger, a print dryer, and a few other things that will give me the most modern setup possible–and most importantly–enable me to work faster. It is costing a lot of money, but I am also earning a reasonable salary. I'm excited June & Phil are coming and disappointed it couldn't be for the opening on April 14th. Today I gave the bank my invitation list (more than 100 names). I also designed the poster which will be hung up all over the Bergstraße promoting it. Ian helped me on his computer. Andrea took my photograph and Claire corrected the wording for it, so I'm getting them all involved. I am working every Friday and Saturday nights plus one or two nights in the week, plus singing in choir on Mondays, giving English lessons on Wednesdays and Thursdays, so I am not exactly around a lot. I have guilty feelings about that, but I'm trying to deal with it. I stayed home with the girls for years (also stayed on my own every weekend for years while Ian was working) so I feel like it's ok to do my thing. Ian doesn't say much. But I expect it isn't easy for him. One of the reasons I started back to work was that I felt totally inadequate and depressed as far as making a financial contribution to our situation. That has now changed and for that I know he is grateful. We are still not out of the red, but we're getting there. I think I mentioned I have lost a lot of weight (25 lbs.) since last May when I started working for the newspaper. I'm sorry I am not writing very often, Mother, but I think about you every day and love you, as you know. And I am so happy these days because I am again doing what I do best! Andrea is working part-time in a photography shop developing color photos. A & C are both into "hippy clothes," bell bottoms & funny tops.

March 17, 1993 - I developed and printed photos from five separate assignments today and have just gotten three more assignments for tonight. It's 4:30 and the assignments are at 6:30, 8:15, and 8:30 in three different towns. So, I'll have to quickly fix something for everyone to eat. June & Phil left a week ago. Andrea has a French exchange friend staying for a week. I have only had two days off since the beginning of January. I've been working on printing the photos for my exhibition. I've got 21 of the 25 printed. The frames have arrived. It has been an incredible amount of work to get the exhibition organized. I have made a mailing of over 125 names and given it to the bank. They have a list of 300 names to send out, too. So hopefully, there will be over 100 people at the opening. The bank is renting a brand new white grand piano and paying DM 400 for a 15-year-old girl, Nina Emery, to play. They're also giving DM 200 to Bernd, an artist friend, who will do an artist talk about me. On March 23rd, it will be 16 years since we moved to Germany. You should take the advice that you have given me most of my life and that is, "get out there and do your best." Sell the house.

April 18, 1993 - The Vernissage - opening reception of my photo exhibit - Ohne Grenzen (translated with double meanings of Without Borders & Without Limits): 25 Black & White Photographs from the Eye of an American of the Bergstraße Over Borderless Europe." I sold three photos at the opening and another one the next morning. I need to sell four more to break even. It was just incredible, better than my wildest dreams. There must have been at least 150 people there which is incredible for an art opening of any kind in the area, so I'm told. But I worked my ass off for the past four months and had invited lots and lots of people. It paid off. Bernd's talk was so good. I had stacks of compliments on what he said about photography in relationship to my background and its influence on my life.

May 12, 1993 - I have not had half an hour to myself in the past two weeks. No joke. No time for housework, garden, Ian, nor the girls. Still, no one is YET complaining. They all know it's not only great fun for me but necessary financially. I sold 10 photos from my show, so I consider it an enormous success. Interestingly, they were 10 different photos. I more than paid for my frames which was my goal. I have been asked to show the exhibit in Heppenheim later this year. Sent info about my flight to CA & Claire's flight to Mpls. Andrea has three part-time jobs, at the weekend she waitresses at the Fürstenlager, during the week she gives a girl English lessons, and one or two times a week she babysits for two daughters of a New Zealand friend of mine. Ian has a new thing going, four different inventions having to do with sailing, which he is hoping will be *THE* thing. He's going to the boat show in Southampton in September.

June 7, 1993 - May was a very successful month, thank goodness as I won't be earning anything in July! My first year back at work has gone very fast. I only hope it lasts, the job and my health as both are vital. We have tomatoes, radishes, strawberries, and red currents...in the garden.

July 30, 1993 - Ian's three new products for the boat show in England in September look *impressive*. Saw them today for the first time. Pray for their/his success!

September 7, 1993 - Ian left for a big exhibition in Southampton with his new brochure of two new inventions, which he also patented, a sailing rig tension setting tool.

October 19, 1993 - You know as well as anyone that we all must do things we don't want to do in life when circumstances force changes. You can't start feeling guilty about moving Grandma to Minnesota so she can get better care. I had another very busy weekend. The small, used Toyota Starlight that I bought is working okay. It's great to drive a small car, easy parking. It is the first car I've bought since I was at the Daily News and the responsibility of it scares me. I'm paying for it over two years, having made a down payment of DM 700. Andrea is also paying DM 2,000 towards it! That is from the money I've saved for the girls each month since moving to Bensheim for the purpose of paying for their drivers' licenses, which is about DM 2,000, and getting a starter car. Andrea passed her theory test last Thursday and takes her practical in November When Claire starts driving, she will also have to pay me the same amount to have the use of the car, we decided. I'm reading the Psalms. I like Chapters 118 and 138. I try to take each day at a time. I would dearly love to get rid of the heavy feeling in my stomach of impending doom. Every day there is such depressing news about the economy in Germany. I don't know when it is going to end.

November 9, 1993 - My Nikon died on an assignment on Friday night. I had three more shoots to do, so I panicked. I used a very old Nikon the whole weekend and turned out some pretty good stuff, amazingly. I have 17 assignments on Sat. from 9 a.m. to 11 p.m. In between, I came home, developed, printed, and went out again. I put Andrea in charge of the food and Claire in charge of the cleaning. No time to even go to the toilet. Today, I'm home sick. I have a dreadful cold and can hardly breathe, sinus blocked, coughing. They called me to work, and I said, I'm sorry, I can't. That's the first time I've said no to an assignment. Andrea takes her driving test on the 11th. I *pray* she passes. Ian is struggling as usual. My good friend, Barbara Jost, who is a General Practitioner in Lorsch, and someone I've given English lessons to for over six years, was in a horrid accident and broke her spine. She will be hospitalized for several months. God help her.

March 8, 1994 - I'm afraid I have some very depressing news. Ian and I have decided we have to sell our house. It is the only way out of our terrible financial pit. The debt at the bank from Anaspec which also has my name on it is DM 700,000. That's over $410,000. I have worried that Ian would drop over dead because of the strain, but he seems to have a strong heart. Unfortunately, it seems in that strong heart of his, there are no longer any loving feelings for ME. He informed me last week that Pat Walker, who has been a friend of mine for over 10 years and who has gone on several exhibitions with him and in fact is helping him one day a week with his sailing business, is also going along on his upcoming sailing trip. I objected. Not because I think they are having an affair. I don't think they are. Yet. I have talked to Pat, an American, who is also having terrible marital problems with her English husband. Ian has sold his land and building but has not yet received the money. It is taking weeks maybe even months. But he does have a new project. Pat has problems of her own admittedly, but I am confident their relationship is still strictly business. I do not think I am being duped. She has heard enough from me about Ian to know that if she went for him, it would be like going from the frying pan (Trevor) into the fire (Ian). Still, I am not so naive as to think that their relationship will remain strictly business under the circumstances. I objected to her going along on the sailing holiday. I said I had never opposed him going sailing with the guys, but when women start going along and I'm not included, that's when I say no. I said if Pat is going, then I'm going. And I said I'd pay for it myself. That is when I was informed that 1. I've ruined every sailing holiday we've ever been on. That was news to me. 2. He doesn't want me to come. 3. He has lost all respect for me. 4. The way I have changed in the past two years, during the time I've started freelancing, is totally negative for him. 5. He doesn't like the way I dress. 6. He doesn't like my hats - which is one of the things that attracted him to me when we met in Moscow, he had told me. 7. I always spoil things when his family is around. That was also news to me. 8. He is embarrassed to go anywhere with me. We haven't done anything or gone anywhere together for months. I know that he does not like the fact that my job is so public. He is totally disinterested in what I do, therefore I don't talk about my work with him. I think that's a shame, because I do so many interesting things and I'm meeting such a variety of fascinating people. What else am I supposed to talk about? We have devoted no time to each other. I am obviously very hurt by his comments and must admit I did not realize that he felt that way. He has treated me like shit for a long time and it has been obvious to the girls and anyone within range of us. Still, I have put it all down to the pressure he has been under for years. I have swallowed a helluva lot. I have concentrated on my job and tried to succeed. And I have done that. What Ian considers negative, in relationship to the changes in me over the past two years, I consider positive. I am more self-confident, self-assured and I'm proud to say, successful. I earned over DM 5,000 in February -the shortest month of the year - that's $3,000! Currently, he is making considerably less. I know that the entire situation has devastated his pride. He probably doesn't like himself much right now and is taking it out on me. I'm the easiest and nearest beating post. We have had money problems since we got married. I am not ready to throw in the towel on our marriage. Incredible though it may seem, I do still love Ian. He must lash out at someone. For the past few weeks, he has been sleeping on the couch. I suggested that we go to counseling. I honestly do not know if he is saying these hurtful things to me because he believes them. He complained about the fact that when he comes home, there isn't a meal on the table. It's been months since I've done anything fun not connected to my work. He said he wasn't interested in doing anything with me and that I should find my own fun. I went to Judy's and cried my eyes out. I don't want to do anything drastic. I am going to try to get through this like all the other bad times, one day at a time. Andrea and Claire are understandably shattered, as you can imagine, when Ian told them we must sell the house. I have lined up another photo exhibit at the Rathouse (City Hall) in Heppenheim May 30 - June 17th.

April 23, 1994 - I sure lucked out when my writing friend at the newspaper, Julia Richter, invited me to go with her to Madrid over Easter. Her daughter had planned to go and had bought a flight and paid for the hotel but couldn't go. Julia said I could come in her place and all it would cost me was my meals. Given I've been so depressed, I jumped at the chance. After going to the Prado, we went to the Ritz Hotel. I had on white jeans and Julia had on black jeans and they wouldn't let us in because we were wearing jeans. The Concierge woman said it was their policy. Looking into the decadent dining room where two "gentlemen" were sitting, one of whom was *wearing jeans*, I pointed to him and asked, "What about him?" She replied, "Oh, he's a guest of a guest." And that was it. We went elsewhere. If my life wasn't so depressing, I'd write more. It's all I can do to get by one day at a time. Some days I'm not sure if I'll make it. I am under so much stress, I'm about to break. I had a good talk with the girls and said we should look at some alternatives to our situation. I just don't know how I can afford to pay for an apartment the size we would have to have plus everything else. I then suggested the idea that one or both could go and live with June to get their high school diploma. I simply cannot leave here right now. I'm doing very well in my job, and I really want to continue. The result of the conversation is that Andrea wants to leave. Claire wants to stay and do her Abitur. I'm sure that Claire having a boyfriend has something to do with that. I am desperate, Mother. One more bit of news. It is very possible I will have to put Duke down next week. For the past several weeks, he has had problems getting upstairs. His legs go out from under him. Something is very wrong with him.

May 18, 1994 - I took Duke to the vet. She said, given my circumstances – I told her I was not able to pay for any long medical treatment – the kindest thing I could do would be to put him down. I decided I needed to do it immediately and that is what happened. It was awful. I was devastated. In fact, I went from the vet's Office to Frau Dr. Woyvode's office where I had my first ever panic attack, crying and shaking uncontrollably. When the girls came home later, and I told them what had happened, Claire said, "You *KILLED* Duke?!" I was a wreck.

May 22, 1994 - It's definite. The girls and I are leaving. I am worried as I will have no money and no car when I come back to MN.

June 21, 1994 - Ian returned from the Boat Show. He's renting space in Kussel, an hour's drive from here. It is cheaper to rent (DM 5 a sq. meter vs. DM 25 here.) There is nothing left of our relationship.

I Will Remain Sane!

I can't believe the words he's sayin'.
After all these years, God knows I'm prayin'.
Gez: I've got to remain sane!

He tells me that he's got no respect.
My work doesn't count, everything is a wreck.
Gez: I need to remain sane!

What about love? I ask him straight.
Love - what's that? - seems it's turned to hate.
Gez: Oh, God! Will I remain sane?

The stress is bad, it couldn't be worse.
Despite hard work, no money in my purse.
Gez: Lordy, I'm desperate to remain sane!

Gotta sell the house, can't see the end,
Don't know if this ole heart will ever mend.
Gez: Please! Will I remain sane?

Think positive is my daily creed
With the power of prayer, I will get what I need.
Have faith I told myself, remain sane!

Gez! Yes, I WILL REMAIN SANE.

Barbara La Valleur, Germany, 1994

NOTE: That was the last letter I sent to Mother from Germany. For the next two weeks, I didn't write any letters because life was a blur. I spent most of those days in bed. Andrea at eighteen, God bless her, became my caregiver making sure I ate something *every day. We had to sell, give, or throw away almost everything we had. Dr. Barbara Jost, came over one day and handed me a check for DM 3,000 (about $5,000 at the time) to help pay for a shipping container so we could take some essential belongings back to the U.S. She told me that she didn't want the money paid back, but that I should "pay it forward" when I get back on my feet and help others out. For the past twenty-six years, I have done my best to fulfill on that promise.*

On July 3rd, 1994, Andrea, oh so willing, and Claire, not so much and I got on a plane in Frankfurt and left Germany. I remember nothing from the flight except opening a present from my wonderful physician, Frau Dr. Waltraud Woyvode, who had given me a package to open on the plane. It was a blank diary to begin the next chapter of my life.

She signed it: Für Barbara, Aufbruch[2], Juli '94

Defining Moment:
Words can hurt. Choose them wisely.

Lessons Learned:
Failure is just a word.

---

[2] *Aufbruch* is the German word for departure. It also points to change. My high school dream of living in Europe was fulfilled. It began like a fairytale and ended like a horror movie. It wasn't supposed to end like that. BL

CHAPTER 8

Nude Number, Circus Caper, Ferry Fiasco

Do one thing every day that scares you.

Eleanor Roosevelt

Nude Number

When the girls were still quite young and in kindergarten, I was making new friends in Germany. It was only natural that I was drawn to the artistic crowd, and while I can't remember exactly how it came about, I found myself befriended by a small group of artists in Pfungstadt. South of Frankfurt about half an hour, Pfungstadt is close to Darmstadt, the German city most noted for being the home of the Art Nouveau movement.

In one conversation, they were commiserating that they couldn't find any live nude models. Most of the artists were working in oils and watercolors. Without much thought, I said I'd be game to model—at the time, I was less Rubenesque than I am now, to be sure.

I went to one of their studios and sat, without shame and, honestly, without a thought that what I was doing would be deemed wrong or inappropriate in any way. Isn't the human body a beautiful object? I was certainly not ashamed of mine. I had a healthy attitude and acceptance of my body.

When I went home later that night, I shared my experience with Ian. I was astonished to learn he was mortified that I would do, as he called it, *such a thing*. Wow! He asked me not to do *that* again. It seemed that I had embarrassed him. While I did not feel the same way, obviously, I acquiesced to his request. I certainly did not want my husband to feel embarrassed for something I had done. I didn't tell him how his reaction affected me, though. We simply never talked about it again.

Upon reflection, it brings up one of the times while living in Europe that I thought the British and American cultures differ. I was learning that Americans are quite prudish in comparison to Europeans in terms of *mores*. In this case, however, although not exactly prudish, there were cultural differences in how we looked at the situation. It was the opposite of what I would have thought.

For example, in comparing TV programs in the two countries, I saw that sex as portrayed in England was far more realistic. In the U.S., people are usually fully clothed or at least mostly clothed despite being in bed–or wherever–while supposedly having intercourse. I found the European attitude in these cases refreshingly authentic, whereas I was beginning to see how the American version was quite unnatural and ridiculous.

It's also a case where we could have learned more about each other had we been able or perhaps I should say *willing,* to discuss it completely.

Unfortunately, we didn't. And that was the end of that.

Circus Caper

A few years later, I had the experience of embarrassing my daughters, Andrea and Claire–although it would certainly not be the last time. I remember their reactions after my caper as clearly as I recall me having had a lot of fun.

They were about nine and ten when a big circus came to the nearby town of Darmstadt, the nearest big city to where we lived. It had many artistic and cultural options, so I was always on the lookout for interesting venues to take the girls. The circus seemed like a fun one.

We were seated high up in the circus tent, I'm pretty sure it was in the top, back row. One of the circus performers shouted out to the audience on his megaphone asking for a volunteer to ride– standing up–on the back of a horse. Being the spontaneous and adventurous person that I am, I waived my hand, perhaps a bit too wildly for my daughters. However, it worked, and I was chosen.

I felt confident I could stand on the back of a horse given I used to stand on my Shetland pony, Spot, while walking around our farmyard. So, I made my way down the bleachers to the circus ring. I must admit to gulping at the size of the horse when I saw him up close. He was probably twice the size of my pony, Spot. Still, I listened as the horse trainer gave me instructions and hooked me up to a harness that wrapped around my middle complete with a hook on the back attached to high wires that would hoist me up so I could stand on the horse, and it would also prevent me from harm, should I fall off. Given the fact that he said the horse would be trotting, I was reassured I'd be okay with that safety measure. Still, it felt like my heart was pounding out of my chest. There were only a couple of thousand people watching, after all.

The circus performer helped me up on the tall horse, which now seemed to have grown taller by the second from my new perspective. It had to be sixteen hands high. We started slow, I balanced, holding the reins, and felt my feet secure under me as the horse walked around the ring. Then my new equine friend picked up speed. At first, I was doing fine. Then, as he started trotting, suddenly, oh, my gosh, I lost my balance!

Thankfully, the safety wire on my back did its job and I found myself swinging to and fro like a ten-pound fish on a five-pound line. The safety wire was gradually lowered, and the horse trainer reeled me in and lowered me to safety. As luck would have it, due to the fact I'd been twisting ten feet in the air, I literally flopped like a fish off the hook-on top of him and we both hit the sawdust in a compromising tangle of limbs.

It only seemed right to continue my spontaneity, so I took his face in both hands and gave him a big kiss on the cheek. The crowd loved it and erupted in applause. We both laughed as we got up, wiped the sawdust off our clothes, and he freed me from the harness.

When I got back to the girls and took my seat, a woman sitting in front of us turned to ask me if I was a setup and part of the circus act? I laughed and assured her I was not.

Andrea and Claire were at the age when nearly everything their mother did was an embarrassment. This episode ranked among their all-time worst "*Mom embarrassed us*" moments.

It was amusing to me that a couple of years later, I was talking with someone who was at the circus that same day who remembered my caper. We shared a good chuckle together.

Ferry Fiasco

We made many great friends during our years in Germany—many of whom, not surprisingly, were associated with the girls' activities and their friends' parents.

So, it was quite exciting when one of my friends, Sue Heise, and I schemed up a plan. You see, both of our families were preparing to drive to England on the same day. Her children, Charles and Lucy, were similar ages to Andrea and Claire. The four had attended music classes and Kindergruppe sessions together, and our families enjoyed dinners at each other's homes now and again. We decided that Claire would ride with the Heises so she and Lucy could play together on the hours-long drive.

We would meet at the ferry terminal in Ostend, Belgium. This was the meeting point where Claire would rejoin Andrea and me as we continued our crossing to Dover and on to see Ian's parents who lived in a tiny village near Canterbury. The Heises would take a different ferry north to Felixstowe and continue their drive to their English cottage in Lancashire.

We'd never done this before, so it seemed like a fun escapade. Claire would enjoy being with Lucy and Andrea and I would have a rare chance for some special time together—just the two of us.

But it *almost* didn't happen that way. It was 1982, years before cellphones were common. I had no way of communicating with my friends that I'd taken the wrong exit on a roundabout and that it had taken me fifteen minutes to get back on the right motorway. We were running late.

Much to my horror, when we arrived at the ferry terminal in Ostend, Claire had already boarded the ferry with Lucy and her family. They were starting to pull up the back gate to close the ferry in preparation to leave the harbor.

But Claire was on the *wrong ferry!*

"Oh, my God! What am I going to do?!" I thought, my mind racing.

In that moment, I realized that I needed to take swift and decisive action to get my daughter off that ferry before she sailed in the wrong direction.

The distance between the two port cities in England was almost one-hundred and fifty miles. That meant I would have to drive through the outskirts of London, almost three hours one way, to fetch her. I couldn't let that happen. What would a seven-year-old girl do alone in Felixstowe for hours before I got there?

My mother instincts took over *big time* and, despite not speaking German well–nor Dutch nor French at all, I ran to the ferry as the enormous car gate began closing. My heart dropped. I couldn't believe what was happening. Clink, clank, THUD! OMG, the gate was closed.

I screamed at the top of my lungs at the attending ground crew: "SHHHHTOP! HALT! STOP! My daughter is on that ferry and it's the FALSCHE [wrong] ferry! Ich muß Sie abholen! I have to get her off!" I'm sure they thought I was crazy if they understood me at all. Still, they certainly knew there was a problem.

It took a few minutes for them to realize what I was saying in my mixed English German screaming rant. But they certainly understood that I was desperate and that I was *dead set on my mission*. After a few minutes, much to my relief, the huge ferry car gate was lowered so that I could go onboard, find my daughter in the three-deck ferry among over 300 passengers and get her off.

I felt bad, momentarily, for causing so many people a delay, but my daughter's safety was my only priority. I had never been so scared in all my life. I also learned that when I set my mind to do something, I could make it happen. I'll always remember the relief I felt when I hugged her. Of course, Claire had no idea of the seriousness of the situation.

When I asked her recently what her memories of that incident were, she said she didn't remember anything about it.

Defining Moments:

I'm not afraid to take a stand for what is right.

Lessons Learned:

When I set my mind to accomplish something,
it happens. I'm intentional.

CHAPTER 9

Scotland: A Close Encounter

It is said that before you die, your life passes
before your eyes. It is in fact true. It's called living.

Terry Pratchett

When our daughters, Andrea and Claire were young, we rarely took holidays of more than a week. So, it was exciting to plan our first, and only, three-week family holiday. The girls were about eight and nine. Little did we know what the future had in store for us. If I had known, I would have had more trepidation than excitement.

We planned to return to Scotland where we'd had a fabulous one-week holiday a few years earlier. I loved the soaring hills with centuries-old stone fences, the many lochs, which reminded me of all the lakes in my home state of Minnesota. The lavender hue of some hills covered in heather is breathtaking. Best of all, the Scottish people are exceptional–welcoming, fun, and interesting. We booked the same holiday cottage we had stayed in on our first trip by Loch Sween near Lochgilphead, about fifty-five miles east of Glasgow.

Despite it being the middle of summer, temperatures were chilly, so it was not uncommon to wear sweatshirts, jeans, winter jackets, and Wellington boots. The first week was spent walking down the pasture from our cottage to Loch Sween to sit near the rocks on the shore watching dozens of seals play in the water. They were fun and noisy. Unfortunately, it wasn't warm enough to go swimming. We explored a few coves and hills where Ian could fly his large model airplanes. One day at the beach we connected with a family who had young children the same ages as our girls. We remained in touch for many years.

Our first unexpected adventure occurred at the end of the first of our three weeks. We had driven Andrea and Claire to Glasgow to catch a plane to London where they would meet up with their cousins, Jennifer, and James. The four cousins would spend a week at a youth adventure camp in Cornwall. We drove away from the airport to head back to our cabin and decided to stop at a pub for lunch. It had been raining and the straight, Roman roads, were slick. Ian was driving our brand-new Volvo estate (the British term for a station wagon), traveling the speed limit when out of the blue another car appeared, and we collided. The other vehicle rammed into the front passenger side of the car which prevented me from opening the door. Thankfully, no one was hurt. But I did have to climb in and out of the driver's seat for the remaining two weeks of our holiday. Awkward.

After exchanging information with the occupants of the other car, we continued to the pub not far away. We were now *undoubtedly* looking forward to a pint (or two). Ironically, or was it fate, shortly after we found a place to sit and had ordered our beer, the couple from the accident walked in. After that first recognition, both parties pointedly avoided eye contact. More than awkward.

Our next unexpected adventure occurred only three days later. We planned to have dinner in a restaurant in Tayvallich, a tiny village tucked near the north shore of Loch Sween. Dressed in our cold-weather gear, we got in the speed boat we'd pulled behind our car from Germany. We had a delightful meal of local fish washed down with a couple of glasses of wine. As we headed back to our cottage, Ian decided to test out the new motor he'd purchased. It was slightly larger but more powerful than the one that came with the three-ply wooden boat. He opened the throttle and away we went, not a care in the world. Minutes later, however, there was a terrific bang. We looked behind us to see water gushing into the boat. Our new life jackets were in plastic bags in the back of the boat.

Ian killed the motor. He stood up, reached behind him, and grabbed two lifejackets. I don't think I've ever seen him move that fast. We put them on in a nanosecond. Before I knew what was happening, he grabbed me and threw me overboard as far away from the boat that he could. He immediately jumped in behind me. He shouted that we needed to get as far away from the boat as possible. As a seasoned sailor, the minute he heard the bang, he *knew* the boat would sink. For him, it was common knowledge that a sinking boat would suck us under, and we would have drowned. Later, I was astounded that he'd had the foresight to grab the plastic bag containing the large novel I had been reading.

As I mentioned, we were dressed in heavy winter clothes. We gathered our wits and determined what best to do. We were closer to one shoreline than the other. Unfortunately, there didn't appear to be any signs of life on that side of the water. There were neither cottages nor people. We had to swim to the farthest side of the loch.

The good news was that where we were was near the cottage in which we were staying. I have never been so scared in my life and for the first time, seriously wondered if I was going to die.

While Ian had been a trophy-winning swimmer in his youth, as a seven-year-old I barely passed my swimming test in Pelican Lake near Ashby, Minnesota. I recall that the swimming test involved being thrown into the lake from a boat just beyond the drop-off. If you made it to shore, you passed. Obviously, I made it to shore that time.

But I digress, back to our dilemma in Loch Sween. My Wellies took on water and made it impossible for me to kick my feet to go faster, which made swimming difficult. So, I had to turn over on my back and paddle the entire way with only my arms. For one hour. Until we reached the shore.

Ian, bless him, kept me calm, followed me, and guided me if I got off course. About a hundred feet from shore, I was petrified to see a handful of seals pop up in the water terrifically close to me. They had heard the loud bang and our yelling. They swam around the cove from their usual spot to investigate. Ian assured me they were harmless and merely curious, which thankfully, they turned out to be. Oddly enough, I was more afraid of losing my glasses than I was of the curious seals.

We reach the rocky shore after one hour of swimming in shockingly cold water. After resting for a few minutes, we climbed through the grass and trees up the hill arriving at our cottage exhausted. We got out of our soggy clothes. I immediately ran a hot bath. Ian got dressed in dry clothes and walked up the lane to inform the owners of our cottage about the accident, as required by law.

The next day we both spent in bed under the covers trying to get warm. Thankfully, we also had a full bottle of brandy which helped. My soggy novel was lovingly dried out and I was able to finish reading it a few days later.

By the end of the week, it was time to head back to Glasgow Airport to pick up Andrea and Claire for our last week together before driving back to Germany. While we didn't encounter any traffic problems coming or going from the airport, we were in for our third surprise adventure upon arriving back at the cottage.

The adage that things happen in threes rang true when we saw as we entered the cottage that we'd had unwelcome visitors in less than the two hours we'd been away. Thieves had broken into our cottage, stolen money, a new camera and, worst of all, broken the fifty pence machine that we needed to provide electricity and heating for our stay. Once again, Ian found himself walking up the lane to the cottage owners to inform them of the break-in. I can only imagine what they were thinking about our "unlucky" family.

The remainder of our eventful holiday went smoothly, thank goodness. That is until we prepared to pack for our return drive back the roughly thousand miles to Germany. You see, on the way over, we had packed the boat full of holiday items which included two of Ian's extra-large model glider airplanes (if my memory serves me right, the largest one had a wingspan of about fifteen feet!) The car was full to the brim. We couldn't see out of the back window and even had numerous items tied to the top of the car. It was, without doubt, the most memorable holiday our family ever had.

Defining Moment:
Surviving is a strong pull for staying alive.

Lessons Learned:
Be prepared – always have life jackets
when you're on a boat.

CHAPTER 10

Mallard Island

Close friends...have occupied a large part of my life
and still do. Whatever the other interests – these
friends know my incurable slant toward primitive
people and wilderness, particularly Indians – who
love droll characters, could probably give you a more
vivid picture of me at this date than I.

Ernst Oberholtzer

My love for our family's home in west-central Minnesota, La Farm, is established. Coming a close second behind is my second favorite place, Mallard Island[3]. This tiny sliver of rocky land has become a slice of heaven for me. This is where I totally relax, am creative with my photography and writing, and where I am in communion with my soul.

A metamorphosis takes place in the fifteen minutes it takes from stepping on the Mallard Island pontoon at Bald Rock and leaving the mainland near Rainier, Minnesota. Once on Mallard, I'm "in the zone."

---

[3] Mallard Island is located just a half mile from Canada out in Rainy Lake, a couple of miles from the Minnesota shore. It's a 290-mile drive, one way, from my home in Minneapolis.

It's not merely the change of scenery as one travels past some of the enormous lake's 2,200 islands. It's not even spotting the bald eagles that unfailingly welcome one back–although that is always a heartwarming sight.

This island is where I experience a sense of spiritual homecoming. I can't explain it, other than to say that on July 19th, 2009, fate introduced me to the place that has taken me on a journey that previously existed only in my dreams.

Given the strong connections and history Mallard has with Indigenous Peoples, I've often wondered if, in a previous life, perhaps I have a connection to Native culture? Since it is well established that the entirety of America was once occupied only by Indigenous Peoples, perhaps that is not so surprising. We are connected over the generations. Once a dear Native elder friend, Anne M. Dunn, a noted storyteller, even gave me the Indian name, Wise Bear.

Nearly every summer (when not overcome by high waters as in 2014 or the Covid-19 Pandemic in 2020), I am one of ten people driving through the beautiful pines of northern Minnesota past International Falls a few miles and parking my car at water's edge near the Bald Rock dock.

As my fellow travelers arrive, groups of two, three, and four gather. We introduce ourselves if we don't know each other or catch up with longtime friends if we do. We all gaze out at the lake in longing as we anticipate the sight of the Mallard Island pontoon whisking us off for our special week.

The two caregivers arrived the previous day to prepare the island and welcome us. Program participants start arriving full of anticipation about the coming week as early as noon on Sunday despite knowing the pontoon's arrival is mid-afternoon. It takes two trips to pick up everyone.

On arrival of the Mallard Island pontoon, I discard my connections to the outside world, transfer my bags of food and suitcase with my week's clothes, camera, and writing materials, climb aboard. I scoot over to make sure there is room for at least three or four others on the seat with their belongings.

As we pull away from the dock heading out into massive Rainy Lake[4], I start to unwind and relax. I can't help but shake my head when I see a scattering of enormous multi-million-dollar homes overlooking water's edge a few minutes from shore encroaching upon the natural landscape being passed. A joyful smile is guaranteed when I see a smattering of small cabins built in the 1930s and 1940s peeking through the pines. They just fit in.

This is where I let go of the tensions from my 290-mile drive, daily responsibilities, the business of life, endless Zoom meetings, and everyday 'lifeing'. We are encouraged to turn off our cell phones for the entire week to experience nature at its finest. The phone reception isn't that great anyway, but I do use my iPhone for taking photos in addition to my trusty Nikon camera.

Over a twelve-year span, it's hard to believe I've only spent a little total of over two months on Mallard. It's as though this place has been a part of my life for decades.

The Review Islands archipelago and their names in English and Ojibwe are Mallard/*Ininishib,* Hawk/*Gekek*, Crow/*Aandeg*, and Gull/*Gayaashik*, all well-known birds in the area. Indigenous Peoples hold the Review Islands as sacred and spiritual.

---

[4] According to Wikipedia, the earliest documentation of Rainy Lake, was known as "Tekamamiwen" shown in French transliterated as "Lac de Tecamamiouen" on an Ochagach map in 1728.

In the 1800s, this expansive lake was used as the voyageurs' highway, linking the Great Lakes to outposts in the remote interior of Canada.

According to the Ernest C. Oberholzer Foundation, they serve to keep Oberholzer's legacy alive by maintaining his library and various collections at Mallard as a retreat and research center, with archives also housed at the Minnesota Historical Society in St. Paul, Minnesota, and the Koochiching County Museum in International Falls.

People familiar with the islands often endearingly refer to Oberholtzer as Ober. Known as *"Atisokan,"* the Ojibwe word for legend or teller of legends, Ober has gone down in history as the torchbearer in the creation of the Boundary Waters National Wilderness.

I love the story of one of Ober's famous adventures in 1912 when he was twenty-eight. He and his friend, Billy Magee, (*Tay-tah-pah-swe-wi-tang*), an Ojibwe, traveled over a two-thousand-mile, four-month journey mostly by canoe. Their voyage extended well beyond Lake Winnipeg–all the way to Hudson Bay in Canada's far north. Wow, think of it! This was unmapped territory at the time and had not been visited by a white man since 1770. As a man who graduated from Harvard, met with Presidents, and traveled the world, it's remarkable that Ober maintained that trip to the magnetic north as the single most powerful experience of his life.

Like me, Ober was also an accomplished photographer. One stark difference between us, however, is that he had to lug all his equipment–huge by today's standards–including an incredibly cumbersome box camera and tripod to get the job done. In addition, he had to bring all the chemicals which he mixed and developed in trays. While I've always had access to a nice clean darkroom during the years I developed and printed my own photos, Ober was challenged to develop and enlarge his photos in the rough outdoors. He typically did that in the evenings while Billy cooked their supper over a campfire. I don't know how in the world he was able to regulate the temperatures which are critical to the chemicals when developing film and enlarging prints. As a testament to his talents, some of those photos hang today on cabin walls on the island more than a hundred years later.

It's amazing how all the unique buildings were made. With the help of Indigenous and non-Indigenous friends, Ober built six sleeping cabins, one tiny meditation building that served as his office and was the first building on the island, a library (which was a boat house in Ober's day), a tool shed, the Wannigan, which was a cook boat from the logging days which he secured to the land and today is the office and kitchen where all meals are served (that aren't on the Wannigan deck or near the fire pit). I find that remarkable given the island is only one and a quarter acre in size.

Three compost toilets have been added in the years following Ober's death.

But I'm getting ahead of myself.

For the programs each summer, I enjoy most the week scheduled for artists, photographers, musicians, writers as well as naturalists and researchers who work on our own independent projects.

In addition, there are three "work weeks" in which dedicated volunteers use their skills to make sure the island is prepared for the summer's visitors. During those weeks, they maintain buildings, gardens, and the archival collections.

Once all the week's participants have arrived, we gather outside the Wannigan (the central kitchen, office and gathering space) standing or sitting next to our piles of belongings at which time the caretakers assign us our sleeping quarters and roommates.

The groups who come to the island for their special week often don't know more than one or two of the other participants. So, there is a brief period of getting acquainted and sharing backgrounds as we walk to our sleeping areas and unpack.

Later, while sitting outside the Wannigan enjoying a glass of wine, we wait for one of the cooks to ring the large bell on top of the Wannigan, signaling the evening meal is ready. It doesn't take more than a day or two for people to become familiar getting around the island and appreciating its awesomeness. We always end up developing life-long friends.

On my first trip, I soon learned the names of each building which reflect their histories, locations, or in some cases, usage. Over the years, I've stayed in each of them, except Ober's House and the Caretakers' Cabin. The island's structures are connected by wood chips or narrow, volcanic-rock pathways up and down the island's hills at both ends.

It is always fun when, after supper and the dishes are done at the end of the day, people make their way to Japanese House to watch the sunset through the screened-in porch. Some visitors claim this as their favorite place for writing because there are so few distractions, although there is only space for one person at a time in the tiny structure. No one complains when the haunting wail of a loon breaks the silence.

During the two separate weeks I learned to play Native American flute, we had 'concerts' at Japanese House most evenings, albeit without an audience. Imagine our delight one night as we were playing when a couple of boats cruised by. Once they heard our flute music, they cut their outboard motors and sat quietly watching and listening to our "concert." They even gave us a round of applause when we finished playing.

That encouragement prompted us to "go on the road" once taking the pontoon, our Native flutes, and a guitar to play songs as we motored through neighboring islands. We received waves of appreciation from people who could hear our flutes as they sat on their lawn chairs enjoying the evening on their docks.

Back on Mallard, once I was walking from Japanese House over the stone bridge to return to my cabin when, for some reason, I glanced over and saw a female loon sitting on her nest. I immediately slowed down, and ever-so-slowly raised my Nikon with its long zoom lens for a closeup shot. As I was about to take the photo, the female loon took a defensive stance and laid prone over her eggs, protecting them. The image I captured remains one of my favorite Mallard photos. Seconds later, she was in the water.

The main attraction for me on Mallard is in the largest structure on the island. Grandmother Drum is honored on the island, after finding a forever home in Ober's Big House in the great room many years ago.

Made in the Anishinaabe tradition, colorful beads creating intricately woven buds, flowers, and vines weave around the weathered leather that covers the drum's top. Worn deer hide strips connect the border's leather and fabric. The wear and tear of years of drumming have resulted in some threadbare patches here and there.

An experience with this Anishinaabe medicine drum left an indelible mark on me after our group listened to a story one evening told by my friend Anne M. Dunn, a well-known, Anishinabeg-Ojibwe grandmother storyteller. Anne was born on the Red Lake Reservation in northern Minnesota over eighty years ago. She now resides outside of Cass Lake close to her children, grandchildren, and other relatives and friends.

As is her storytelling tradition, she had shared with our group one of the stories passed on to her by her mother and grandmother.

One by one, each of us went up to Grandmother Drum. When it was my turn, I slowly approached Grandmother Drum and stood while Anne spoke softly to me. She told me that I share a special connection with the drum. Although she did not explain further, I was left having had one of the most spiritual experiences of my life--resulting in shivers running down my spine. I couldn't explain it and I will never forget it. I've thought about that so many times. I have an inexplicable connection to Grandmother Drum.

In translating the indigenous name of the drum, *Minisinaanakwadook,* "*Minis*" means "island" and "*Inaanakwad*" refers to clouds. The suffix "*ook*" tells us that she is female, a grandmother drum who we are told has made her home on Mallard Island and wishes to reside there to protect the islands. I always feel a sense of peacefulness when I am in the presence of Grandmother Drum. [5]

The first two times I went to Mallard, I stayed at Front House. One year, while taking photos of the huge boulders just outside, I captured an extraordinary view. I clearly see a profile of an Indigenous person in the largest boulder with flowing hair reaching back to touch the water. There are even what appear to be white tears running down the cheek. To my knowledge, no one else has ever seen this image before or since, possibly due to the fluctuation of the water levels differing from year to year. That photo, which I call Guardian Spirit, has become my all-time favorite Mallard photo of the thousands I've taken over the years. It certainly added a soul-filled love and appreciation to my Mallard connection.

---

[5] Chi Mii Gwech, Minisinaanakwadook translated is Big Thank You, Mother Drum.

Another memorable photo I took shows an ethereal image that I say depicts the spirit of Frances Andrews, Ober's friend who for many years took up residence at Front House during the summer months. Clearly visible is an outline in the shape of a person which occurs to me as the spirit of Frances Andrews, especially since I took the photo on the side of Front House where she stayed for so many years.

Front House is where the Aurora Borealis, also known as the Northern Lights, are often first visible in the night sky. The first person to see the vibrant greens and various waving colors move across the sky runs to the Wannigan to ring the bell even if it's in the middle of the night. No one wants to miss that extraordinary experience.

My first stay on Mallard was when my late sister, Sharon Henneman, invited me to join a group of Storytellers and Drummers. I had recently retired and was finding my way through my new existence of being "refired" vs. retired. I was blessed the following summer to return along with a few of the same women, so we continued the tradition of telling our stories and beating our drums together.

During the time between those two trips, one of my best friends, the late Linda Hutchinson, and I spent a day making our own handheld drums – under the helpful guidance of Doris Linder of ReadEagle Drums in rural Henning, Minnesota so we could bring them along the following and subsequent years. Now and again, I enjoy looking through the photo book I made of the drum-making experience.

Having grown to absolutely love the island, I wanted my husband to have the experience and, perhaps, come to understand how and why Mallard is so special to me. I encouraged him to join me for a Work Week in the spring of 2011. He wasn't disappointed.

He pitched in to help with the construction of a new drainage tile system for one of the buildings. We stayed at Winter House and enjoyed the big round oak table on which we played Hand and Foot, our favorite card game.

Later that summer was the first year I joined a group learning the Native American Flute for a week with Jon Romer. While Jon is not an Indigenous person, he worked for years teaching music at Bug-O-Nay-Ge-Shig School operated by the Leech Lake Band of Ojibwe in Bena, Minnesota. He has played and recorded Native American flute music for appreciative audiences for over three decades, often playing at Native events and ceremonies. I enjoyed a second week the following year and expanded my skills at Native flute playing for an additional week.

In 2014, a flood prevented the summer's programs. However, in 2015 and 2016, I particularly enjoyed my time during Individual Artist Week in which I stayed in tiny Artist House on my own and loved it. It was there that I researched, created, and later self-published the photo book about the Frigate Friday[6].

My dear friend, Maryann Chowen joined me in 2017, in Bird House. She had joined me during an earlier trip. I thought as someone who was half Native (mother) and half German (father), she would really appreciate Mallard.

Due to both knees being replaced in 2018, I was not able to navigate the rocky paths and gradations of Mallard's landscape and was not able to walk down the steep hill to Japanese House. Still, it was a relaxing time of reflection, reading, and writing, and, of course, friendships. I admired my friend, Maryann, who had to

---

[6] Frigate Friday, a two-story houseboat, was moored at Gull from the earlier 1980s until its demise in 2011. My photo book of Frigate Friday can be found on the island's Wannigan collection.

climb a ladder to get to her room on Bird House's top floor to work on her artistic projects and beadwork while I was on the middle floor.

One year, I discovered a fascinating area behind Bird House that I hadn't noticed before. Imagine my surprise when I discovered a whole area among the trees that looks nothing like the rest of the island. It is resplendent in gorgeous, velvety mosses and lichen-covered rocks right down to water's edge. You can even find native wildflowers if you are observant. It was fun to photograph the vibrant flora and fauna shades of green.

Tiny Artist House surprised me the first year I stayed there. Given I'm a gregarious person, I was amazed at how cozy and special it felt to be alone for a few hours a day and was very content with my own company. I loved the skylight. Although each place has given me a unique experience, if I had to choose, I'd say Artist House is my favorite place to stay on Mallard.

On my last trip in 2019, as well as two other years, I was back in Cedar Bark for my sleeping and workspace. I love sleeping with the sound of lapping water all around. Pure heaven! I remember one afternoon taking photos and short videos of the pouring rain as it splashed against the window and the water below. Talk about relaxing, oh, my. I lost track of writing in the logbook where each year, residents are encouraged to write a few lines or a page in each of the cabins' journals. It is so interesting to read what people have written about their experiences. The journals themselves are works of art with poetry, carefully written prose, sketches, watercolors, and amusing tales. All true, of course.

There are so many descriptive words I could use to describe this amazing place: peaceful, powerful, photogenic. Tranquil, transformative, timely. Meditative, adventurous, nature-filled, rustic. Then there is the incredible light at dawn. I never complain about getting up before sunrise when that dazzling sun starts peeking over the horizon and shows itself on the easterly end of Mallard. Everywhere I look, I see photographic possibilities.

I mentioned earlier, the best sunset views are from of Japanese House's screened porch. There, one gazes upon the sky-blue pink especially after a beautiful still sunny day, from horizon to horizon and between the islands. It's easy to become lost in thought. The best place for viewing and photographing sunrises is sitting on or near the rock formations where I photographed Guardian Spirit at the east end of the island.

One week, our group of women was honored by a spontaneous ceremony celebrating the four directions. Standing outside Ober's House on the highest point of the island, my friend, Maryann, whose father was a talented Indigenous artist (and whose mother, of German heritage, was a dedicated Registered Nurse) told the story of the Medicine Wheel - the Great Spirit Gitchie Manitou. In the ceremony, she designated pairs of us to represent animals from the four different directions (north, south, east, west). Eagle was from the East, Coyotes from the South, Bear Spirit from the West, and Buffalo from the North. Again, it was another soul-filled, spine-chilling moment.

It's not all sunny or even warm weather on Mallard, as can be expected in the far north of Minnesota. After all, Minnesotans are sometimes called the Frozen Chosen as we are a stone's throw from the Canadian border. Still, even rainy or cooler days are welcome. There's no urgency, nowhere to go, and nothing to do but relax, breathe, and enjoy.

When the weather warms up, I love getting into my swimsuit and grabbing a floating ring, then stepping gingerly down the rocky steps outside Artist House into the calm, cool water. I'm not a swimmer, I'm a floater. It's been told that some people have even gone skinny dipping late at night.

I've gone canoeing, or rather more accurately, I've been in a canoe and have taken photos, while appreciating others who do the work of paddling and maneuvering deftly through the water between and around the islands.

As I mentioned, taking photos is a large part of the islands' allure to me. Bird watching, especially on the balcony of Bird House or even in one of the chairs on the deck of the Wannigan or Cedar Bark, is also a favorite pastime where you can see any number of warblers, sparrows, hummingbirds, Red-Eyed Vireos, great blue herons, and Chickadee. In spring, there is a Loon Nesting sign posted at the west end typically within sight of Japanese House at water's edge.

There, I've watched a loon sitting on her eggs, hoping for a chance to see them hatch. At first, two then one egg was left after a beaver or muskrat had, unfortunately, had an egg meal. Although I've never witnessed an egg hatching there, the soulful call of the loon is my favorite sound - whether on Mallard or at La Farm. Some lucky people have seen bear and even bear cubs as well as beavers, which I have seen on the islands. Other animals in abundance are deer, fox, hares, grey squirrels, voles, mice, turtles, frogs, and toads. Bats are not uncommon among the white Cedar trees. Somehow, it is always magical to see wildlife so close.

The last time I was there, I saw a young whitetail doe hop the shallow short distance between Mallard and Hawk Islands near Ober's House. What a thrill!

One year, my timing was perfect for blueberry season. They are found on the hilly path to Front House. There was the perfect amount for Minnesota artist Faye Passow to make two pies for our evening meal. Delicious!

Taking in the aroma of the island, the smell provided by pine and cedar trees - especially after a light rain–that delicious, heaven-sent fragrance can startle my amygdala. Another aroma comes from a flaming firepit by Cedar Bark, which on occasion inspires an early riser to create an incredible breakfast of bacon and eggs cooked over the open fire.

So, always well before I'm ready for the week to end, dang, it's Saturday morning. Time to tidy my living space in preparation for the next person, pack my belongings and head down to the Mallard Island pontoon, typically waiting for the last group of kindred spirits to leave.

I wonder why is it that this trip always seems to take less time than the arrival trip six short days prior. Back on the Minnesota mainland, I stop at Charlene Erickson's home, pay her the nominal sum of five dollars a night for parking on her property and head home, memories intact.

As I head through the tall pine trees on the narrow road back to catch the main road to International Falls, I reflect on the Ojibwe belief that parting is never final, I silently whisper *Giga-waabamin miinawaa* ~ I shall see you again.

Defining Moment:
I found a slice of heaven on Mallard Island.

Lesson Learned:
Instead of 'goodbye', Ojibwe people say *giga-waabamin miinawaa* or I shall see you again, reflecting their belief that parting is never final according to Professor Anton Treuer, a Native American pioneer in revitalizing the Ojibwe language. My sentiments exactly when I leave Mallard.

CHAPTER 11

Famous People

It is the lives we encounter
that make life worth living.

Guy de Maupassant

While I can't claim to be famous, I've been most fortunate to meet or be in the presence of numerous famous people in my seven and a half decades. I'm not sure what it is, or if it's solely me who feels this way, but when I meet or see a well-known person face to face, it's always a thrill. Perhaps it is because I admire them for their talents, accomplishments, or beliefs. Whatever it is, the experience makes my heart skip a beat and leaves me smiling. So, it's a positive experience. And while I didn't have a conversation with each one of them, I had "run ins" literally or figuratively with many of them. Even more exciting is that I was able to photograph many of them.

My first experience with a famous person was when I was fifteen. I attended one of Bobby Vee's first concerts in Fergus Falls, Minnesota. Bobby Vee was a handsome young man and popular Minnesota singer in the early 1960s. I was lucky enough to be standing in the front row at his concert when a button fell off his sweater. I had a tiny sewing kit in my purse and sewed it back on right then and there. I wonder how many fifteen-year-olds today would have a sewing kit in their purse?! A few years later, my older sister, Sharon, would have the future Mrs. Bobby Vee as her college dorm roommate.

My next experience with a famous person was three years later during our senior class trip to Minneapolis. It was only the second time I had traveled to the "Big City." Our class had two choices of events to attend that evening: a Minnesota Twins baseball game or the inaugural week production of Hamlet, a Shakespeare play directed by Sir Tyrone Guthrie. Although I wasn't lucky enough to personally meet Sir Tyrone, as the director, he was in one of the front rows of the audience, so I did see him. I was one of three senior girls who attend the play along with my favorite high school English teacher, Miss Vivian Ramberg. I credit Miss Ramberg for teaching me the love of the English language. All our other classmates went to the Twins game. I never regretted going to the play and still have the program to this day.

My President John F. Kennedy (JFK) story is, perhaps, a little more poignant. I spoke of it in an earlier chapter. JFK, as he was fondly known, was a bigger-than-life figure who was immensely popular. With his beautiful wife, Jacqueline, and their two small children, Caroline, and John-John, they had captured the world's collective heart. In fact, the nickname for the Kennedy Administration, pointing to its glamorous, media-culture image, was Camelot.

During the nine years it took me to obtain my four-year college degree, one of the things I'm most proud of was being one of four founding members of the Institute for Minority Group Studies at what was then called Moorhead State College (MSC). The four students represented Native Americans, African Americans (now Black is a more politically correct term), Chicanos (as we referred to Latinos in the '60s), and Caucasians. One of our goals was to bring speakers representing different cultures to our predominantly white campus to expand our understanding of their histories and cultures.

Since I was the only one of the four students who owned a car, I became the go-to person to pick up speakers when they flew into Fargo's small Hector Airport across the river in North Dakota from our campus in Moorhead, MN. Dennis Banks, a nationally, if not internationally known Native American activist, was the most famous person I had the privilege of picking up and driving to campus. My memory of that experience and our conversation is, unfortunately, gone with the years. What I do remember was the proud, self-confident, and bold, unwavering stand for his people.

The most famous person I interviewed during my years as a staff writer at The Forum of Fargo-Moorhead was former Vice President Hubert H. Humphrey (HHH), who had recently completed his term as vice president. HHH had been highly admired by my parents and grandparents for decades. I, too, looked up to his leadership, integrity, and passion for social justice. Imagine my shock when the editors at The Forum chose me - a young cub reporter - to *fly* to Minneapolis and interview Humphrey and write an article about his new position as a university professor at the University of Minnesota and Macalester College.

My interview took place in the back of his huge, black limousine. It was just HHH and me. With notebook in hand, I asked my questions and wrote down his answers. He took his time answering them and spoke eloquently. What I remember most about that interview, though, was when he asked his driver to pull over as we drove by a school playground full of squealing children. Thankfully, I had the presence of mind to be silent while he spent several minutes focused on the children and smiling before he told his driver to go on. It was a moving and powerful experience. The article I wrote for The Forum is one of the most cherished newspaper stories of my career. I even had it laminated so I could preserve it.

After graduating Summa Cum Laude as the first person to major in Mass Communications at MSC (now called Minnesota State University, Moorhead), in the dead of a freezing Minnesota winter, I set my sights on a warmer climate. The world was my oyster, as the saying goes. As ridiculous as it sounds now, at the time, it was common to browse media magazines for job openings. No Google, no internet at the time.

When I saw a small advertisement for a position as Editor of *Carib Magazine*, a weekly tabloid-sized newspaper in Charlotte Amalie, in the U.S. Virgin Island, I jumped at it! Perfect. I called the number and spoke with Sen. Earl Ottley, the owner of the weekly newspaper called *Carib Magazine*. He not only owned the newspaper, but he was also a senator in the Virgin Island government. I literally "sold myself" over the phone telling him I was "the perfect person, just what you're looking for!"

It turned out to be an extraordinary experience in more ways than one. On that phone call, I explained to him that since I had recently graduated and didn't have any money. Would he please provide me with a plane ticket? I had become bolder since my Starbuck, MN, days, for sure. He complied, sent me the ticket to the island via a stop in New York City, where I was to meet him in his hotel. We would have dinner and he would turn over keys to the office.

The next day, we were to fly off in different directions, me to my exciting new job on the island and him to Washington D.C. for political meetings. What a night! After I checked into the hotel, we met at the restaurant on the main level. While I don't remember the meal, I do clearly remember the conversation. When he handed me the keys to the office, he explained that Ruth Smith, his office manager, would pick me up at the airport not far from the office in downtown Charlotte Amalie. I asked how she would know who I was. He assured me that wouldn't be a problem. Left somewhat confused, but trusting he knew what he was talking about, the next conversation was one I will never forget. He invited me up to his room. Red flags flying, I looked him straight in the eyes, smiled, and said, "Senator Ottley, thanks, but no thanks. I don't need to sleep with anyone to get where I'm going," and that was that. I left the restaurant and went up to my room. Alone. I didn't see him again until he was back on the island some days later and we met in the office. He never made another pass.

Coincidently, it was Carnival week on the island when I arrived. Imagine my amused surprise when I entered the airplane to take off for my island dream job and saw that I was the only white person on the plane. All the other passengers were islanders who lived and work in NYC and were going home for the week's carnival festivities. To this day, I don't know if Senator Ottley was testing me to see if I'd sleep with him as a way of knowing how I'd get on with my job on the island whose majority of residents were Caribbean islanders with dark skin. Or if he just wanted sex that night and I happened to be there.

Years later, I was back in New York City on my way to the former Soviet Union for the first time. I was having lunch with a girlfriend at the popular restaurant adjacent to the Rockefeller Ice Skating Rink. As we were eating, we glanced over to a nearby table and saw Peter Lawford, Frank Reynolds, and Soupy Sales. That was a brief, but exciting encounter.

Over the years, I had the joy of attending concerts or lectures featuring well-known actors, singers, musicians, and authors including Debbie Reynolds, Joe Cocker, Bette Midler, Toni Morrison, Susan Voss, Ellen Snortland, William Kent Krueger,

Kent Nerburn, Dr. Elvis Franscio, and Nachito Herrera. I still tear up every time I hear Bette Midler's song, *"From a Distance."* It was popular when I lived in Germany. It made me so homesick thinking about my family back in the states.

Toni Morrison's lecture at the University of Minnesota years later was also a memorable experience. You knew you were in the presence of greatness when she walked in the lecture hall even before she said a word. She is a veritable powerhouse.

Susan Voss, a Minnesota comedian, and friend of my sister's was always good for an entertaining evening. She made me laugh.

I first met Ellen Snortland over the phone, having been introduced by a mutual friend. A native of South Dakota, the Californian is an actress, advocate, and author of *Beauty Bites Beast*, a must-read about how to protect yourself from assault. Ellen wanted to perform her one-woman play in Minneapolis. She asked if I'd like to be her producer. Since I was retired, (although I prefer to consider myself Refired), I agreed, without knowing exactly what a producer does nor what my accountabilities would be. You probably know by now I am a risk-taker.

Of course, I had never produced anything, let alone a play. I soon learned that, at least in this instance, the definition of a producer was "putting butts in seats." I'm proud to say that for the one-week run of *Now That She's Gone*, I filled the Pangea World Theater production every night.

William Kent Krueger and Kent Nerburn are two of my favorite Minnesota authors. Krueger is an American novelist and crime writer best known for his series featuring Cork O'Connor, set mainly in Minnesota.

Kent Nerburn is an American author originally from Minnesota. Nerburn has published sixteen books of creative non-fiction and essays, focusing on Native American and American culture and spirituality. He won a Minnesota Book Award in 1995 for *Neither Wolf, Nor Dog*, and again in 2010 for *The Wolf at Twilight*, both of which I highly recommend. After reading his books for years as well as being Facebook friends with both him and his son, Nik, a talent in his own right with film and photography his artistic expressions, I had the opportunity to meet both at the Kaddatz Gallery in Fergus Falls. It was the opening of a series of Nik's photos. Now living in Oregon, Kent Nerburn's books always leave me with thought-provoking ideas and principles.

Meeting William Kent Krueger was quite a different experience. When I was Executive Director of a non-profit keeping seniors out of nursing homes on the East Side of St. Paul, MN., one of our seniors was Kent's amazing father. I remember on my first visit with him, he asked if I'd ever heard of William Kent Krueger. When I said no, he got up, went to a different room, and brought back Kent's first book in the Cork O'Connor series, *Iron Lake*. He proudly said, "Kent is my son," and offered to loan me the book. I've since bought not only Iron Lake, but every one of his 22 books. He has become one of my favorite authors. Our paths have crossed several times as he lives in the Twin Cities where I live. He's also made presentations at my place of worship, Westminster Presbyterian Church (WPC), where his books have been the subject of our annual All-Church Read. Recently, I had the incredible privilege of interviewing Kent Krueger about his newest book for the monthly series, *Speaking of Authors...*, a new gig I started in 2021 interviewing authors. Those programs are available on YouTube.

Dr. Elvis Franscio, a former Mayo Clinic singing doctor from Haiti, caused a social media sensation when an iPhone video of him went viral as he played the piano and sang with a fellow physician in the Mayo Clinic Gonda Building Atrium. A few months later, I was having my second knee replacement surgery at Mayo Clinic in Rochester, MN. When my surgeon, Dr. Michael Stuart, the co-director of Mayo Sports Medicine Center, came to check up on me the day after surgery, Dr. Elvis was his accompanying physician. Having seen the video of him singing on Facebook and then on The Ellen (Degeneres) Show, I recognized him immediately as "the singing physician." His bedside manner was every bit as great as his singing voice. He even did a selfie with me that I posted on my Facebook page.

Then there is Nachito Herrera a world-famous Cuban pianist who lives in Minnesota and who I am proud to call my friend, along with his incredible wife and manager, Aurora Gonzales. I saw him perform and then he and Aurora joined Westminster Presbyterian Church (WPC), where I am a member. I was honored when he played at the opening of an art exhibit at Cubano Gallery in Golden Valley, MN, owned by Michael Appleman, Ph.D. I was the only non-Cuban artist, showing sixty of the photos I'd taken while on a mission trip to Havana and Matanzas, along with our senior pastor, Dr. Tim Hart-Anderson, and a group of WPC members.

In 2020, when Nachito fell victim to COVID-19 and was hospitalized for weeks, I was one of a handful of WPC friends who met on Zoom daily for weeks to support Nachito's wife and daughter, Mirdalys Herrera Tweeton, who sings with him. Eventually, Nacho returned home to continue his recovery. He was unconscious for two weeks and nearly died. I'm convinced the power of prayer played a part in his miraculous recovery.

The only well-known sports person I recall meeting is Tony Oliva, the Cuban-born right fielder who played his entire fifteen-year career with the Minnesota Twins. Oliva is a friend of Nachito's, so it was not surprising that he appeared at the art opening at the Cubano Gallery at our opening. Oliva also attended an extraordinary concert Nachito gave at WPC later that year. Always a front-row person, I had the honor of sitting next to Tony and Gordette DuBois, his lovely wife of over fifty years.

My husband, Arnie Bigbee, and I have been social justice activists for many years. While we don't go on marches nor to demonstrations like we did when we were younger and pre-COVID-19, we have marched many times in support of Indigenous Peoples every spring to remember the hundreds of Native women who have been abducted and killed and remain lost to their families, their bodies rarely, if ever, found.

Here are some of the famous activists I've met over the years in addition to Dennis Banks whom I mentioned earlier. Although Nicholas Kristof is a well-known journalist who has been a columnist for the New York Times since 2001, he is also an advocate and frequent speaker at major venues around the world. He and his wife, Sheryl WuDunn, are the first married couple to win a Pulitzer Prize for journalism for their coverage of China's Tiananmen Square protests. Their book, *Half the Sky*, is a compelling read about turning oppression into opportunities for women worldwide. Kristof was one of a long list of world-famous speakers at WPC's nationally known *Town Hall Forum* which always fills our beautiful and historic downtown Minneapolis church with thousands of people and is broadcast live over *Minnesota Public Radio*.

Another WPC Town Hall Forum speaker I am blessed to have heard and met is Brian Stevenson, the Black attorney who single-handedly fought and saved 140 people from death row. The founder of the Equal Justice Initiative, Stevenson spoke about his book *Just Mercy* which later became an award-winning movie starring Jamie Foxx as Stevenson.

Will Steger and Josie Johnson are two more activists I've met and photographed. Steger, of course, is the formidable voice calling for "understanding and preservation of the Arctic and the Earth" according to Climate Generation, his legacy non-profit website. An educator, author, entrepreneur, and documentarian on the effects of climate change, Steger is known for leading the first confirmed 1,600-mile dogsled trip to the North Pole in 1986 without re-supplying. He, too, was a speaker at a WPC Town Hall Forum. His message is clear: climate change is real and if we don't act now, there will be dire consequences for humanity and, in fact, the earth on which we live. Wake up, people!

Not surprisingly for an international photojournalist, I've admired and looked up to famous people in my field. I've met and photographed a few journalists like Nicholas Kristof. Then there is the local NBC affiliate, *KARE 11's* Boyd Huppert. He is known for his weekly feature called *Land of 10,000 Stories*, a play on the Land of 10,000 Lakes for which Minnesota is well known (despite the state having 11,842 lakes.) I attended a speech by Boyd when he spoke about his life as a farm kid who became a well-known and respected television journalist. His Minnesota stories often end up as the uplifting story at the end of NBC's *Nightly News* with Lester Holt.

Katie Couric and Tom Brokaw are two media icons I have admired for decades as setting high standards in journalism. I met Katie Couric when she spoke at a University of Minnesota alumni event a few years ago, while Tom Brokaw was another WPC Town Hall Forum Speaker. I was able to capture photos with both.

Then there is Minnesota's own Garrison Keillor. I first met Keillor in 1994 after I returned from Europe and was volunteering for a candidate who was running for the U.S. Senate. We had listened to *Minnesota Public Radio's Prairie Home Companion* in

Germany for years and I'd bought his books and tapes. I pride myself in taking a decent photo of Keillor, one of those individuals for whom a good photo comes seldom. A few years later, after his fall from grace due to an unfortunate incident in which he was accused of inappropriate behavior toward a co-worker, my husband and I attended a dinner theater where he performed his dry humor stand-up routine. We thoroughly enjoyed him.

Last, but most certainly not least, are several politicians I've met and/or known over the years of local, state, regional, and national importance. I've already mentioned my experience with JFK. Next would come President Bill Clinton and First Lady Hillary Rodham Clinton. That's quite the story!

It was one of the most comical experiences I have ever had. It was September 1994, two months after I returned from Germany.

Before I started back to work full-time, I wanted to ease into the American way of life–which was vastly different from what I'd been experiencing for the past two decades. I decided to volunteer full-time for the Democratic endorsed candidate, Ann Wynia who was running for a seat in the U.S. Senate representing Minnesota.

When I walked into Wynia's volunteer campaign office, I was directed to Marlene Kayser. I would soon learn she was a volunteer extraordinaire, and she oversaw the campaign office. When she asked me what my background and skills were, I told her I was a photojournalist and had recently freelanced full-time for seven German newspapers. Her eyes lit up. She promptly put me in charge of the White House Press Corps of international journalists who would be accompanying President Clinton to Minneapolis *twice* before the November election. The President's headquarters would be at the Hilton Hotel in downtown Minneapolis.

Two young "advance" women oversaw the "*Minneapolis White House*." They trained me to run a special teletype machine and showed me the duties I would be performing. There were strict instructions about the all-important RED PHONE, which was for Presidential use ONLY in case of a national disaster. They gave me the schedule of events hour by hour and further explained my other duties. And that was pretty much it. In retrospect, it was hilarious that I was put in that position, having been out of the country for two decades. Unlike most Americans who had watched these people in the media for years, I didn't know nor recognize any White House staff. Nor did I know any of the high-level Cabinet members mingling in the hotel suite all around me. Had I known, I'm sure I would have been "star-struck"!

On the day President Clinton and the First Lady were in Minneapolis, I had been invited by the two young advance women to come to the underground garage from which the President's motorcade would be leaving. They were headed for an appearance with Ann Wynia at a local college.

Although I wasn't informed *why* I was there, I inwardly *expected* it was so I would be able to personally meet and shake hands with the President and First Lady. The two advance women and I were chatting in an area of the underground garage waiting for the dignitaries to pass through when someone urgently requested their presence. They dashed away in mid-sentence, and I was left standing alone to await their return.

In less than a minute, a Secret Service man came rushing up to me. He asked me in a pressing voice what I was doing there. I answered honestly, "I don't know," as the two women in charge hadn't explained anything to me. He immediately took me firmly by the arm, apologizing while looking around for a place to "secure me." He discovered a small room nearby and whisked me inside. I looked around the tiny room which had a small table, a chair, and not much else. The window was covered with a Venetian blind. The

Secret Serviceman commanded, "Stay here!" I meekly asked if it was okay if I peeked through the blinds so I could get a glimpse of the President. He reluctantly said "okay" with the caveat, "*But don't open the blinds!*" With that, he left and locked the door behind him.

There I was, fifty years old, climbing on top of a fragile table in the bowels of the Minneapolis Hilton Hotel peeking through the Venetian blinds. If anyone had seen me, I'm sure it would have been quite a sight!

After a few minutes, the President and First Lady passed in front of my window–literally twelve inches on the other side of the glass - and in a second, they were out of sight, climbing into their limousine and driving out of the garage. At that point, the Secret Serviceman came back, unlocked the door, and apologized profusely.

The two women had, by then, returned and were unaware of my banishment but invited me back to the Presidential Suite where we watched the President and Ann Wynia speak on television. We feasted on the huge uneaten breakfast which had been intended for the President and First Lady. It was a banquet fit for a President for sure and could easily have fed a couple of dozen people. It was seriously over the top: a fruit basket with apples, oranges, bananas, kiwis, pineapple, a selection of *eight* different kinds of cheese, a similar number of cold meats, three different types of eggs, hard rolls, soft rolls, croissants, whole wheat bread, bread for toasting, coffee, tea, orange juice, grapefruit juice, tomato juice. All this for the President and First Lady, not the staff. I couldn't help but think of all the hungry people in the country. Crazy!

At the risk of seeing the food go to waste, I asked if I could take some of it back to Ann Wynia's campaign office for the volunteers, to which they generously agreed.

Then I explained to the two young women what had happened in the garage. They realized they had neglected to have me go through the "Presidential clearance channels" after which I would have been given a special lapel pin designating me as a "safe, cleared person." We had a good laugh and as a "consolation prize" they gave me the bottle of "Presidential" wine and a lapel pin with President Clinton's signature which I still have. That evening while watching the news of the President's trip to Minneapolis with my sister, we gave a toast to Ann Wynia and the President. Unfortunately for Minnesota, Ann Wynia lost the election. But the experience remains one of the most memorable and funniest of my life.

My relationship over the years with Brig. Gen. Clara Adams-Ender has been an endearing one. What a powerhouse. I was first introduced to her when I was working as Communications Coordinator for the University of Minnesota School of Nursing. I had also been doing freelance work for the international nursing magazine of the nursing sorority, Sigma Theta Tau International. The magazine editor assigned me to photograph and write a cover story about Gen. Adams-Ender. I not only flew to Washington DC to cover her story, but she also graciously invited me to stay with her and her charming German husband, Heinz Ender.

Clara had obtained her master's degree in Nursing from the University of Minnesota years before. She is a retired U.S. Army Officer who was Chief of the U.S. Army Nurse Corps from 1987 to 1991. A woman of numerous accomplishments, awards, and firsts, she was the first woman to receive a master's degree in military arts and sciences from the U.S. Army Command and General Staff College. She is also the first African American nurse corps officer to graduate from the United States Army War College. When she retired in 1993, she was a Brigadier General and commanding officer of Fort Belvoir, VA. She was named a Living Legend by the American Academy of Nursing, not bad for one of ten children who grew up on a tobacco farm in North Carolina. Years after my interview with Clara, I was honored when she flew to Minneapolis to attend my wedding to Arnie. We have seen each other several times over the years when, as a distinguished alum, she returns to speak and take part in University of Minnesota events.

In July 1995, a year after returning to my home state, I had my first personal encounter with the late John and Annie Glenn. It was my fiftieth birthday, and I was having a few friends over for a party. So, when the telephone rang, I expected one of my guests was going to ask for directions or tell me they'd be late to the party.

Imagine my surprise when the voice at the end of the line said, "This is John Glenn." My first thought was, "Ja, right," someone was pulling a birthday prank on me. Still, I asked unbelievably, *"THE John Glenn*?!" "Yes," he responded quite jovially. My sister, Dr. June La Valleur, had shared with him that it was my birthday. "My wife, Annie, and I heard it was your birthday, so we thought we'd call and sing you Happy Birthday." You could have pushed me over with a feather. They chimed into singing a happy birthday duet with gusto and in harmony. We chatted a little, but I was so excited I can't remember what we talked about. Little did I know then that our paths would cross in person a few months later in Washington D.C. I had never been to the nation's capital. I jumped at the opportunity to accompany my sister and her friend, Jill Schwimmer, when they invited me to go along that fall.

While they were attending different meetings, I walked, took the Metro, visited museums, and explored the amazing historical sites of D.C. It was one of the most memorable weeks ever. When Senator John Glenn, D-OH, learned that we were visiting the area, he invited us to come to his office and promised us not only a tour of the Senate Chambers (including a behind-the-scenes view rarely seen by regular tourists) he would also take us to lunch at the famous Senate restaurant.

On the day the three of us were to meet Senator Glenn we were walking around looking for the place to go when a tall, Black woman was about to pass us in a large hallway. Since we didn't know where we were going, I stopped her and said, "You look like you know where you're going. Could you please help us?" She pleasantly gave us correct instructions for where to go. A few minutes later, Jill, who was very active in politics, asked me, "Do you know who that was?" When I said, "No," she said, "*That* was Senator Carol Moseley Braun!" Wow, another brush with fame. Sen. Moseley Braun is the first African American female elected to the U.S. Senate in American history, the first African American U.S. Senator from the Democratic Party, the first woman to defeat an incumbent U.S. Senator in an election, and the first woman U.S. Senator from Illinois.

But back to Senator Glenn. He had gained worldwide fame on February 20, 1962, when he became the first American to orbit Earth (three times) for four hours and fifty-six minutes in the tiny Mercury spacecraft Friendship Seven which is now housed in the National Air and Space Museum in Washington D.C. After meeting with Senator Glenn in his office, during which each one of the three of us was able to speak separately about what was important to us, he took us to lunch where we enjoyed the Senate restaurant's famous, tasty bean soup and then we went on a Senate Chambers tour. He took us "behind-the-scenes" and showed us the table on which the Declaration of Independence was signed over two hundred and forty-five years ago. We cautiously touched the table. *What a thrill!* Our special time with Senator Glenn resulted in an incredibly generous invitation the following day to join him and

Annie on their custom-built yacht, Pura Vida, for an entire day in Chesapeake Bay.

We met Annie the next day when they picked us up at our hotel and drove us to Chesapeake Bay, Maryland. You would never have guessed that we were in the presence of one of the most famous couples in the world. Annie, his gracious, diminutive wife, who for years suffered from a stuttering disability, was a giant in her own right as a champion who advocated nationally for years for people with communication disorders.

We spent the day relaxing and taking in the gorgeous sights of Chesapeake Bay. Later, while the yacht was moored, we relished a delicious meal of crab legs at one of their favorite restaurants on the bay. Joined by the crew for lunch, we were even able to take home the small wooden mallets used to break open the crabs. Back on board, we received a thorough tour of their precious Pura Vida and I was even allowed to steer the boat for a while (under the watchful eyes of the captain). Oh, my! While I've had sailing holidays on thirty-six-foot sailboats in Greece's Ionian Islands a few times, that was incomparable to their three-story watercraft which included two large salons, four staterooms, and a two-man, full-time, year-round crew. I will always remember that special day with fondness and the generosity of John and Annie Glenn.

Senator John Glenn died in 2016. He and Annie had been married for seventy-three years. I was saddened to learn about Annie's death from COVID-19 in May of 2020 in an Arden Hills, MN, retirement home. She lived to be a hundred years old. She remains the most gracious person I have ever met.

Coming from a politically active family specifically, members of the Minnesota Democratic-Farmer-Labor (DFL) party whose candidates my parents and grandparents had always voted for, it wasn't surprising that I, too, became involved in politics upon return to the states.

Some of the well-known Minnesota politicians I've met and supported over the years are (in addition to Vice President HHH, about whom I've written) are, Vice President Walter Mondale, Senator Paul and Sheila Wellstone, Senator Amy Klobuchar, Senator Al Franken, Governor Mark Dayton, Governor Tim Walz, Senator Tina Smith, former Representative and current Minnesota Attorney General Keith Ellison, Senator Melisa Franzen, Representative Betty McCollum, and Representative Dean Phillips. Most of them I've met several times either at fundraisers, like the one my sister, Dr. June La Valleur, and I held for Minnesota's Amy Klobuchar for her first run in the U.S. Senate, or at political rallies.

In 2019 when my husband and I were invited by the MN AARP to meet with Rep. Dean Phillips in his new office in Minnetonka, we were told we had fifteen minutes to discuss our topics. As luck was on our side, during our meeting his next appointment was canceled and we were able to spend over an hour talking with Rep. Phillips, who was cordial and very engaged. I couldn't help but notice all the bare white walls in his office suite of rooms which they had moved into the previous week. I offered to provide some of my Minnesota photos to add interest to his walls. He graciously accepted. I currently have seven photos exhibited in his office, six of Minnesota and one of the Dr. Martin Luther King Memorial, Out of the Mountain of Despair, a Stone of Hope carved by sculptor Lei Yixinin, in Washington D.C.

Once in the mid-1990s, I had a private meeting with former Republican Gov. Tim Pawlenty when I was Executive Director of the Payne-Phalen Living at Home/Block Nurse Program (LAH/BNP). The purpose of the non-profit program on the East Side of St. Paul was to keep seniors safe in their homes with the support of neighborhood volunteers. I took one of our special seniors, Chuck Aguirre, one of ten Latino brothers who had served in the military. We were there to advocate for increased funding for our program. I had written proof that our small non-profit program, one of forty-five LAH/BNPs, a unique healthcare model for seniors in Minnesota that would save the state over *four million dollars* in one year if the MN Department of Human Services would support our grant request of *fifty thousand dollars*.

Although that wasn't our only funding, it would have made *THE* difference to our survival. While Gov. Pawlenty was gracious and smiling during our meeting, and despite our having been acknowledged by two national organizations for our work (the American Alzheimers Association and the National Alliance for Hispanic Health), our grant was not approved. The program soon was doomed to an untimely end due to lack of funds. I was heartbroken. That experience, sadly, led to my early retirement.

I can. I will. Watch me! was the mantra for *Oprah Winfrey's 2020 Vision: Your Life in Focus* that toured the country in January before the 2020 COVID-19 lockdown. That mantra not only resonated with me but also with the other eighteen thousand mostly women at the Xcel Energy Center in St. Paul. Never had I paid so much to see anyone - $178.63 for my seat on the main floor, *thirty-three rows back*, but in view of the stage. Oprah commanded the stage walking and talking, microphone in hand, with such ease that I felt like she was having a personal conversation with me. She followed her own advice and became focused on her message: balance of mind, body, and spirit. Later in the afternoon, Oprah welcomed her friend, Tina Fey, to the stage to thunderous applause.

A video from the previous day was projected with the two friends paying homage to their "Shero" by tossing their hats in the freezing air in front of the famous downtown Minneapolis attraction, the Mary Tyler Moore statue. After an hour-long conversation with Fey, Oprah also introduced two friends in the audience, Tamron Hall, nationally known broadcast journalist and TV talk show host, and Suze Orman, author, financial advisor, and tv host. It was a fun day to remember.

A few weeks later, Arnie and I attended a program at the University of Minnesota featuring Gloria Steinem, one of my longtime "Sheroes" and not long after that, we took in a presentation by Rick Stevens, internationally known travel guru who spoke about his favorite European travels.

Defining Moment:
It has been said, you define the moment,
or the moment defines you.

Lesson Learned:
When an opportunity arises, seize the moment.

CHAPTER 12

Heartbreaking

*The shattering of a heart when being broken
is the loudest quiet ever.*

Anonymous

I've been blessed with a good life. I'd even go so far as to say
it's been quite an extraordinary one. That doesn't mean I haven't had
my ups and downs. It's just that I've had more ups than downs. I've
done a lot of things and gone to a lot of places. I have few regrets.

There are three events I have had in my seventy-six years that
I'd call heartbreaking. Each one was different. Each one involved a
close relationship. They are my divorce from Ian, the estrangement
from our adopted sister, and the sudden death of my older sister, Sharon.

I've written about the end of my twenty-year marriage to Ian.
That was heartbreak number one. In retrospect, the process was
quite swift, taking less than a year to unravel what had been, in my
experience (for the most part) a wonderful life for over two decades.
Sure, we had our highs and lows and certainly struggled with the
lack of money most of those twenty years. But we had more high
times than low, I thought.

The breakup of our marriage eventually resulted in the girls
and I leaving Europe where they were born in England and grew up
in Germany. I had the job of a lifetime freelancing full-time as a

photojournalist for seven German newspapers. Moving back to Minnesota, where I had my family support system was our best option and I don't regret that.

The three of us moved to Minnesota, where I'd grown up, but the girls had only visited their relatives a few times. We were welcomed by my oldest sister, June, who had a huge Victorian house in one of Minneapolis's nicest neighborhoods and was living on her own. My mother, God rest her soul, bought a used car that was waiting for me when we arrived. We lived with June until the girls completed high school and were in college. Her generosity in allowing us to live with her gave me time to get back on my feet and start earning a living.

The hardest part of adjusting back to single life was that the man I'd loved for so long would no longer communicate with me. That cut me to the core. I wrote letters to him although I don't know if he ever read them. It was raw heartbreak. I cried and cried and cried.

Communication has been one of the most important things to me in my adult life. Although our marriage was over, I will always love Ian as the father of our daughters.

The heartbreak was a wound that would prevent me from dating for over five years. Thankfully, though, I did eventually, find a soulmate when I met and four years later married, Arnie Bigbee. On November 26, 2021, we celebrated our sixteenth wedding anniversary. Arnie loves me unconditionally. I am blessed. Life is good.

The second heartbreaking event of my life occurred over a few years through a series of events and, oddly, non-events. It started on October 27, 1996, when my two sisters and our third cousin, Claudia, also a La Valleur, bought La Farm. Her father, "Red" and our father, "Bud," were first cousins and, are buried next to each other in the rural Presbyterian cemetery a few miles from La Farm.

As I've written in a previous chapter, La Farm is a parcel of thirty-three acres of what is left of our grandparent's farm where they lived from 1920 to 1960. The four of us created The La Valleur Sisters Trust when we bought the farm. The following year, after discussing the idea, our mother legally adopted Claudia on September 26th, traveling to Iowa with Sharon to deal with the legal aspects of the adoption. The judge said it was the first adult adoption he'd ever presided over of someone of that age. Claudia was in her fifties. Now, the four of us were "really sisters" or so I thought.

We enjoyed time together at La Farm. We had celebrations and fun crazy parties inviting friends and neighbors to events like a "Poor Taste Party" where guests dressed and brought food in poor taste. We had a "High Tea Party" with guests who were required to wear gloves and hats.

Claudia's third husband had died a few years later and within months, in August of 2011, she married again. We liked her new husband, Dave. He was quite nice, and we were so happy for them. But it didn't take long for things to change. Significantly.

It's not unusual for newly married couples to want to spend time together, but it was soon apparent that it would be a mutually exclusive relationship between only the two of them. They each disposed of their own properties so they could buy a home together. That wasn't surprising. We didn't mind buying out her portion of La Farm to support her. In fact, because of La Farm, they were able to live there for a few months while disposing of their individual properties and buying a place of their own.

What was surprising, is that within a short period of time they would disengage not only from us and La Farm, but with her girlfriends also, who told us they rarely saw her as well.

To this day, I don't know of a specific occurrence that happened to warrant such a split, but eventually we didn't see them at all. They stopped coming to La Farm. They didn't call. They were never available to come to La Farm when we were there. They'd be on a weekend trip somewhere. Eventually, there was no communication. It was hard to understand. I was deeply hurt.

The third heartbreak also cut deeply for a different reason. My sister, Sharon, two years older than me, died suddenly of an aortic dissection. I'd never even heard of that medical condition before. Growing up, we were very close, riding our ponies together in the summer on the farm where we grew up only a few miles from La Farm. We had pretend coffee parties at the back of the house sitting at our little red metal table and chairs. We had incredible conversations in the boughs of a huge oak tree we called Old Smoky in the woods behind our house.

We had so much fun together and sometimes got up to mischief, like the times in the fall when we would sneak Mother's cigarette 'butts' that we had been collecting all week to smoke when Ron and Gerald Larson came on Wednesday nights. That's when the boys' father would stop by our farm to pick June up for church choir practice and drop the boys off for a few hours. We'd sneak up to the top of the corn piled in the corncrib and sit on the hard cobs of corn smoking and coughing.

Sharon had visited me when I lived in Europe, along with Mother and June at various times. Since returning to the states, we all grew even closer, having bought our grandparents' farm which we lovingly call La Farm, a play on the family name. We had so much fun together there the first few years.

Sharon knew me better than anyone else in the world. We were very close.

So, when she died suddenly on February 21, 2017, I was devastated. It took me months to get over it. Still, after years, I often forget she's gone and go to call her and share moments of joy or sadness.

The bitter part of Sharon's death is that a few months before she died, in the politically contentious year of 2016, Sharon voted for a different person for President. As I wrote earlier, we had been lifelong active Democrats for at least three generations, and I couldn't believe she supported a person whose values were so diametrically opposed to those with which we had grown up. Plus, in my opinion, her candidate was a despicable human being without morals and an affront to women.

Sharon and I had a few tense weeks of not speaking to each other, which was the first time in our lives that had happened. After the election, and before Thanksgiving that year, we sat down together at La Farm and talked it out. We agreed that I would not bring up all the things I hate about "it" and she would not attack the media, of which I am obviously a member. Basically, no talking politics.

I wonder what she would have said about the unthinkable insurrection at the Capitol by white national extremist T-supporters that took place on January 6th, 2021.

Sharon's strong fundamental Christian beliefs included staunch views against abortion as reasons for supporting her candidate.

During the time after that national election until her death, our relationship returned to a loving one, talking on the phone weekly and spending time together at La Farm. But it would never return to that solid closeness that it had been before. To me, that is so damn sad.

For me, the heartbreak caused by Claudia was worse than what I experienced with Sharon's death. Sharon didn't *choose* to die. It happened. Claudia *chose* to disengage and leave the family. I still don't understand it. The experience has cut me so deeply. That is truly sad.

Defining Moment:
Life is a mystery.

Lesson Learned:
I was willing to have my heart broken again
for the privilege of loving and being loved again.

CHAPTER 13

Landmark

At all times and under all circumstances, we have
the power to transform the quality of our lives.

Werner Erhard

The weekend of March 3, 1995, was pivotal. That is when I first participated in the Landmark Forum and began a life of transformation.

A year earlier and across the ocean in Europe where I'd lived for twenty years, everything around me unraveled. During that time, my oldest sister, Dr. June La Valleur, did The Forum, a three-day and an evening transformational education course.

Despite everything disintegrating in my world in Germany, multiple and supportive long-distance phone calls with family pulled me through. June seemed different somehow, softer. I wasn't sure if it was because my mind didn't seem to be functioning on all cylinders or what. Growing up with June, my oldest sister, she always seemed to be very much in control. Any argument she had she would always win because she would always be right! In fact, she even argued with a road sign once on a family trip, which ironically had somehow been turned. Of course, she was right.

So, as I prepared to return home after two decades living abroad and we were on these calls, I began to sense something different in her voice, I asked her about it. She shared that she had recently participated in a transformational educational program called The Landmark Forum. I was curious, but too preoccupied with my own problems to think more about it.

Once I returned to Minnesota with my two teenage daughters and we had moved into June's lovely three-story mansion – at least that's what I called it – in one of Minneapolis' most exclusive neighborhoods, Linden Hills, I witnessed first-hand the transformed June. She was calmer, more relaxed. Gone, too, was that edge, the righteousness that I felt when we would disagree, even about minor things, in the past. Now, she was there, in the present and listened.

I knew that I needed to regain my self-confidence and return to some sense of normalcy and especially to restore my soul. June referred me to a psychologist colleague. My therapist said it would probably take a few months of therapy and medication to begin with. Then I remember her saying I would probably be on that medication for depression the rest of my life. She clearly didn't know me. I told myself, "Just wait. I'll show *you!*" I was able to stop taking medication and completed therapy within five months before the end of that year. The following March, I was mentally ready to experience what had now become a keen interest in the program June had completed.

What was this program called *The Landmark Forum* all about? I had learned it was ontology, the study of being of human beings. I was eager to find out more, so I registered to do the program. I walked into a nondescript office building in Edina, Minnesota, and sat down. Jerry Baden, I guessed to be fifty-ish, not very tall, and with squinty eyes (especially when he smiled), walked to the front of the room. He was one of fifty Landmark Forum

Leaders around the world who leads the inquiries that look at what it is to be human and how life works.

For three days and an evening, I joined about a hundred and thirty people: men and women, younger and older, all kinds of professions, trades, educational backgrounds, and mostly white. Jerry walked across the stage encouraging people who wanted to share to raise their hands. He called on participants one at a time to come to the microphone and share their life experiences, and what they wanted to get out of their participation.

The Forum, simply said, is a three-day ontological conversation broken up into several conversations based on distinctions developed by Landmark, about how life works. It is the foundational program for the many other transformation educational programs and seminars that Landmark offers.

Throughout the weekend, there were times during which we would pair with the person sitting next to us and share with them our responses to questions Jerry asked. It didn't matter that we didn't know the other person. By Sunday evening, we were all connected; through listening to each other, our experiences, our conversations as well as through looking at what was of interest and important to us.

Each participant had filled out a form before the course stating what they wanted to accomplish out of their participation during the weekend. Most people not only succeeded in reaching their goals, but they also experienced breakthroughs beyond their expectations. They were able to see things from their past that had "stopped them" in life. Everyone got what they came to accomplish and most people, by Tuesday evening at the end of the course, said that the experience had exceeded their expectations.

I don't remember precisely what I wrote on my form. The previous year had been traumatic. I had left our wonderful home and garden in Bensheim, my great job freelancing full-time for seven

German newspapers, and all my dear international friends. That had left its mark on me, and I still felt a sense of loss. I know I wanted a closer relationship with my daughters, although we got along fine. In addition, I wanted to be able to be free from my past, so I could create a new future to live into. And that is exactly what happened.

Over the years, I have attended numerous seminars and programs and even led Landmark introductions, programs, and seminars. In addition, I have been on staff four different times for different lengths of time. Currently, I am facilitating courses in a senior division of Landmark called the Wisdom Division. One of the key practices of facilitating is listening. Wow! I'm learning more about listening in this program than I did while in college in my communications program. Powerful.

Once COVID-19 became a pandemic, Landmark's programs, like most of day-to-day business, went from in person to virtual through the Zoom platform. Ironically, one of the results of that transition is that people from around the world are now able to participate in programs that previously were impossible without living near where the programs were being offered. In the courses I'm now facilitating, people are from coast to coast, across Canada, Europe, Australia, and New Zealand.

One of Landmark's key distinctions is, "Without integrity, nothing works." I have found that to be true in all of life. Whenever I find something not working in my life, whether it's with a relationship, a project or a goal, I look at my integrity.

In the intervening years, as you have read in these chapters, I successfully completed my career and am happily "refired" as I prefer to call retirement.

My two daughters graduated from high school, obtained degrees in their chosen fields, are successfully engaged in their respective fields and are homeowners. They are happy, adjusted and living full lives, with Claire and her fabulous husband, Cliff Shaw, and my sweet grand dogs, Rudi and Birdie, in Minnesota. Andrea, having recently moved from Barcelona, Spain, where she had lived for five years, just bought her first house in Woodway, Texas, the state of my mother's birth.

I'm blessed to have married a wonderful man, Arnie Bigbee, we still have a loving relationship despite living virtually 24/7 for almost two years through the Pandemic.

I've given back to my community by serving on the Edina, Minnesota, Arts and Culture Commission as well as Chair of Public Art Edina. Arnie and I enjoy volunteering in various ways at Westminster Presbyterian Church in Minneapolis. He also enjoys volunteering with AARP and lobbies for social justice and affordable housing issues.

After Sharon died, buying La Farm with Claire, the La Valleur family farm near Ashby, Minnesota, was an extraordinary accomplishment. As was buying La Condo, our home in Edina, Minnesota, with Arnie before we married sixteen years ago. Both events far exceeded my expectations and dreams.

Over the past few years, I've had numerous photo exhibits in Minnesota, North Dakota, and Iowa. Two years ago, I was inducted into my hometown Battle Lake (Minnesota) Education Foundation Hall of Fame, an enormous honor.

Arnie and I went for a hot-air balloon ride on my sixty-fifth birthday even though he's not that keen on heights. I created a beautiful self-published photo book to remember that special balloon ride. To top that off, the next year, I jumped out of an airplane at 14,000 feet on my sixty-sixth birthday. Simply said, I have gone after and achieved whatever I wanted in life, no matter the risks.

I credit my participation in Landmark's programs plus the love and support of my family and my faith community for my successes in the past twenty-six years.

Landmark lists the Seven Top Benefits of the Landmark Forum that participants have when completing the course as:

- Courage
- Self-Confidence
- Freedom from resentment and regret
- Peace of mind
- Ability to fully express your love
- The ability to make decisions without doubting yourself
- Happiness

I gained all of that and so much, much more. Over the years, I have shared and supported hundreds of people registering into The Landmark Forum. People who are interested in living a life they love, people looking for a new sense of freedom and power and people interested in communicating more effectively will achieve all of that. Perhaps, more important than anything, though, is the peace of mind that results for people.

I remember my heart bursting with love after I completed my first weekend. Landmark gave me hope for world peace. It is certainly the best experience that I have ever had to gain access to a world that works for everyone. Who wouldn't want that?

For the past two years, I've been trained as a facilitator which is a program leader for the Wisdom Division as well as being a Custodian for the Social Commons. As a Custodian, I co-host inquiries about life in the Zoom platform. These conversations are

55 minutes, free, and open to anyone who is a graduate of the Landmark Forum and the Wisdom program.

To learn more about and register into The Forum and subsequent programs, visit www.landmarkworldwide.com. My tip is to take a seat in the front row. You won't be sorry.

And to June: Thank you, sister, I am forever grateful for everything.

Defining Moment:

The first time I did the Landmark Forum I learned I don't listen well. For the past 26 years, I have made it my mission to become a better listener. Being a Facilitator and a Custodian for the Social Commons in Landmark's Wisdom Division is the best training for listening (and listening to the end) that I've ever experienced.

Lessons Learned:

It is important that you get clear for yourself that your only access to impacting life is *action*. The world does not care what you intend, how committed you are, how you feel or what you think, and certainly it has no interest in what you want and don't want. Take a look at life as it is lived and see for yourself that the world only moves for you when you act.

Werner Erhard

Epilogue

The view is clear in the front row.

Barbara La Valleur

One of the satisfying achievements in my life was learning German, thanks to my kindergarten-age daughters. It wasn't as difficult as I imagined it would be. Words are pronounced like they look, not like the propensities of the English language with our myriad of "silent letters" and different sounds for the same letters.

Another advantage of German is their practical use of stringing words together to make new words like Vergangenheitsaufarbeitung, which translated means "working off the past." That's basically what I've been doing the past three and a half years while writing my memoir, although working is not how I would describe the process.

It seems more like reviewing my past. What I have attempted to do is to give you, the reader, a sense of my exciting and adventurous life. Perhaps you will take away an idea to try - or not!

I always wanted to reach the age of one hundred so I'm intending to live another twenty-five years or so. However, to my knowledge, not one of my relatives has reached past their early nineties, so that may not happen. What I do know, is with the time I have left, I certainly plan to live each day with design and aliveness.

The purpose for me in writing my memoir is to leave behind my story of a life of possibilities. I hope to inspire others to do things that are outside of their comfort zone. Go skydiving, like I did on my sixty-sixth birthday. Travel, as I did, all over the U.S. and Europe. The world is a big, yet small place. You can go anywhere, anytime if you put your mind and resources towards your goal. When you fall, dust yourself off and rise to new adventures. None of us is guaranteed anything in life except that we will die. So, before that happens, love your family and love your friends. Show them. Tell them. Take a seat in your own front row.

Defining Moment:
"I don't count."
That was a belief I made up about myself at age seven when I asked a question that revealed my aunt's hand during a card game – a big no-no.

Lesson Learned:
I do count. I finally realized during the Landmark Forum fifty years later that so many of my decisions in life were based on a misguided belief.

About the Author

Barbara La Valleur moved from Ashby to Battle Lake, Minnesota, in the summer of 1960. Her late mother, Elva Evander, owned Elva's Beauty Salon for a number of years until she moved the shop to her home at Camp Roma on Eagle Lake where she lived with her late husband, Loyd Evander.

That summer, Barbara won the door prize at a used car dealership opening in Battle Lake. The prize was a 1937 Chevy which she sold to a friend for $50 and bought a typewriter from Dick Tamke at the Battle Lake, Minnesota, Review. That launched her career as a photojournalist for 55 years including a few years freelancing full time for seven German newspapers.

Barbara graduated from Battle Lake High School in 1963 among the top 10% of her class and had the distinction of being Class Clown along with her classmate, the late Bruce Noyes.

She attended Moorhead State College, now Minnesota State University Moorhead, working her way through as a Staff Writer at The Forum of Fargo-Moorhead, a Pulitzer Prizewinning newspaper, graduating in 1972 with very little college debt. Her first job was as editor of Carib Magazine, a weekly newspaper in the U.S. Virgin Islands. From there, she went to the Daily News of Wahpeton-Breckenridge as Chief Photographer. She was the only woman Chief Photographer of a daily newspaper in the entire upper Midwest.

During her years at the Daily News, she received numerous first place awards from the N.D. Press Women in photography, editing, writing, layout and editorial column. At the invitation of Soviet Press Women, she went with 80 women journalists from the U.S. on a life altering tour of Moscow and Leningrad (now St. Petersburg) in 1973. The following year, she moved to England, was married, and had two daughters. The family moved to Germany where they lived for over eighteen years.

She returned to Minnesota in 1994 along with her daughters, Andrea, and Claire. For the next several years she worked at various positions including as Communications Coordinator of the University of Minnesota School of Nursing and as Executive Director of a St. Paul non-profit.

She also continued to freelance with her photos and articles appearing in various publications including the Star Tribune, The Forum, Women's Press and an international nursing magazine. For the past 10 years, she has self-published 20 photo books and has devoted much of her time volunteering for her church, her community and Landmark Worldwide, a transformational educational company.

Following her passion for art, she served six years on the Edina Arts and Culture Commission and was Chair of Public Art Edina expanding the rotating sculpture exhibit with a regional reputation. In April 2017, she received the Mayor's Individual Service Commendation award in Edina, Minnesota, for "outstanding and exceptional volunteer service to the community."

The past three years she has focused on solo photo exhibits in Minnesota including at the Germanic American Institute, St. Paul; Edina Art Center; Kaddatz Galleries in Fergus Falls; Evansville (Minnesota) Art Center; First Universalist Church in Minneapolis; Westminster Gallery at Westminster Presbyterian Church,

Minneapolis; The Red Door Gallery, Wahpeton, North Dakota and Pearson Lakes Art Center, Lake Okoboji, Iowa.

Her exhibits include photographs of Europe, the U.S. especially Minnesota, a mission trip with Westminster Presbyterian Church to Cuba, and her life's work. In the future, she hopes to bring her unique exhibit of 25 Black and White Photos of European Women in Traditional Male Professions and Trades to Bensheim, Germany, where most of the photos were taken while she was a freelance photojournalist with seven German newspapers.

Barbara has been a contributor to tpt (Minnesota Public Television's NextAvenue.org), with a series of photo essays about art teachers. She is a contributor to WINK, an international literary magazine with several front and back cover as well as inside photos. She was a public art consultant for a major public art project in Edina and is a public speaker. She also writes an occasional blog at www.unheralded.fish/author/barbara-la-valleur/.

Currently, her Cuban photos are on exhibit at Cubano Gallery in Golden Valley, Minnesota, believed to be the largest gallery of Cuban art in the upper Midwest. She is the only non-Cuban and only photographer exhibiting. She is a member of several art galleries in Minnesota and North Dakota.

Barbara lives with her husband, Arnie Bigbee, in Edina, Minnesota. They each have two daughters and together they have three grandchildren and three grand dogs. Barbara and Arnie are well known in their community for their volunteer work. They have co-chaired the Minnesota ACLU fundraiser, volunteered for over twenty-six years for Landmark Worldwide, an international transformational education program as well as their church, Westminster Presbyterian Church, for social justice and affordable housing.

She owns La Farm, a 33-acre "piece of paradise" near Ashby, Minnesota, with her younger daughter, Claire Shaw, the Broker in Charge and a real estate agent at the Keller Williams office in Uptown, Minneapolis. La Farm is part of the original farm of her grandparents. She and her family spend as much time as possible at La Farm throughout the year. Her other daughter, Andrea La Valleur-Purvis, is a Principal Product Designer and Creative Director. She recently moved from Barcelona, Spain where she had lived for five years, and now lives in Woodway, Texas.

Printed in Great Britain
by Amazon

25545944R00106